THE ART *of* PRICING

THE ART
of PRICING

HOW TO FIND THE
HIDDEN PROFITS
TO GROW YOUR BUSINESS

RAFI MOHAMMED

CROWN
BUSINESS
NEW YORK

Published in the United States by Crown Business, an imprint of the Crown
Publishing Group, a division of Random House, Inc., New York.
www.crownpublishing.com

Crown Business is a trademark and the Rising Sun colophon is a registered
trademark of Random House, Inc.

Library of Congress Cataloging-in-Publication Data
Mohammed, Rafi.
The art of pricing : how to find the hidden profits to grow your business /
Rafi Mohammed.—1st ed.
Includes index.
1. Pricing.   2. Strategic planning.   3. Consumer satisfaction.   I. Title.
HF5416.5.M64 2005
338.52—dc22   2005010609

ISBN-13: 978-1-4000-8093-9
ISBN-10: 1-4000-8093-2

Printed in the United States of America

Design by Lenny Henderson

10   9   8   7   6   5   4   3   2   1

First Edition

To my family,
thank you for your care, support, and friendship
throughout the various phases of my life.

Contents

Preface

Every company I've met has had hidden profits. By hidden profits, I mean that through better pricing, they could increase profits and generate growth. The notion of better pricing often makes people uncomfortable because they assume it means taking advantage of customers by charging high prices. As you are about to see, better pricing does not have to be so draconian and can actually create win-win situations for both consumers and businesses. My perspective on pricing for profits and growth is really about offering customers a variety of pricing options and allowing them to select the one that works best for them.

The goal of this book is to discuss pricing, a key business strategy that many companies struggle with, in an easy-to-understand manner. The clear and friendly writing style that I've tried to create shouldn't be interpreted as "Rafi's only discussing the basics of pricing." On the contrary, the concepts in this book range from the fundamentals to state-of-the-art. These tools will allow you to identify and capture your product's hidden profits.

As with any challenging project, I had good and bad days while writing this book. On more mornings than I care to admit, it was a struggle to face the prospect of spending another full day on research and writing. However, some afternoons were truly magical. It was thrilling to come up with a new insight or write a particularly clever passage. I find the deeper I dig into pricing, the more fascinated I become with it. In this spirit, I'd love to hear your opinions on the ideas in this book as well as your own pricing experiences.

Rafi Mohammed
Cambridge, Massachusetts
RafiMo@gmail.com

THE ART *of* PRICING

CHAPTER 1

Hidden Profits

Pricing for Profits and Growth

My friend David Straus has always been interested in cooking, not just as an avocation but as a career. He's followed the tried-and-true career path of other successful chefs: attending culinary school and cooking at a variety of restaurants. Dave combined all of these experiences into a unique style of cooking and shares a trait that distinguishes the great from merely good chefs: he cooks to please his customers. So it wasn't a surprise when he recently called to tell me that he was opening his own gourmet restaurant.

After catching up with each other, Dave shared a business problem that he was struggling with. "Rafi," he said, "I don't know what prices to set on my menu." With a hint of exasperation, he went on to wonder aloud, "Should I price the prime strip steak with morel mushrooms at eighteen or thirty-one dollars? How will the thirteen-dollar difference affect the number of customers that patronize my restaurant?" His pricing decision was further complicated by conflicted feelings of "not wanting my restaurant filled with just a bunch of rich people; I want to serve a more diverse group of customers. But then again, I am in business to make a profit."

What's interesting about Dave Straus's pricing dilemma is that it reflects a fundamental challenge faced by every business in the world—from small startups to Fortune 500 companies.

I've had the good fortune to work on pricing issues in academia, government, and the private sector. As an academic, I wrote my Ph.D. dissertation, published new ideas in top research journals, and taught classes to budding managers on pricing. As an economist at the Federal Communications Commission, I worked on deregulating local and long-distance telephone rates as well as on public-policy issues that use price subsidies to make telecommunication services affordable to the poor. Today, I work with companies of all sizes in a wide range of industries on their pricing strategies. Throughout all these experiences, I've found that the root of pricing problems at most organizations is the same: they don't think about pricing in the right way.

For most people, pricing is an unsettling exercise involving a mixture of compromise, fly-by-the-seat-of-the-pants analysis, guessing, marking up costs, following competitors, and doing things as they've always been done. What usually results is a price that "just works." Eighteen- or thirty-one-dollar decisions compromise at $24.50. What's the difference between using a price that "just works" and one derived from my pricing for profits and growth philosophy? A lot of hidden profits. The potential benefits of pricing extend far beyond making simple, black-and-white, $18 or $31 decisions.

Continuing my conversation with Dave, I pointed out that his desire to expand his clientele beyond rich diners actually touches on my central idea about pricing: some customers will value your product more than others will. For example, budget-minded young couples with a mortgage and kids who want to celebrate their anniversary with a fancy dinner can't afford to pay as much as the well-to-do who delight in dining at the best restaurant in town. This simple realization—that customers place different values on the same products—empowers companies to price for profits and growth. The right way to think about pricing is as a series of strategies that serve (and capture different profit margins from) customers with different product valuations.

After an hour of discussing Dave's business, goals, and potential customers, we designed a set of pricing strategies for the restaurant. They included early-bird specials; senior citizens' discounts; regular menu prices; $200 annual "charter" memberships that provide a 25% discount on all meals for a year; discounted three-course meal bundles; a lower-priced bar menu; and premium-margined chef's-table seating. Of course, the restaurant will make lower profits from those ordering early-bird specials compared to the margins gained from high rollers willing to pay for the privilege of sitting at the chef's table and hobnobbing with the creative genius behind the meal. But this is exactly what pricing for profits and growth strives to accomplish. The right set of pricing strategies enables companies to serve (and profit from) as many customers as possible.

When I visited Dave six months later, he was beaming with pride at how well his restaurant was doing. He took particular delight in serving, through his early-bird pricing specials, those diners who normally could not afford to enjoy gourmet meals. As I looked around the packed dining room, I was happy for my friend. Dave had done a great job of pricing for profits and growth. Profits were being enhanced by options like chef's-table seating, and the early-bird specials were growing his customer base. Think about all the hidden profits Dave would have missed out on had he viewed pricing as an $18 or $31 decision!

This book presents a pricing for profits and growth philosophy that's relevant for any service or product, as well as for any type of business—domestic or global, large or small. The reason for its universal applicability is the simple fact that for every product in the world, there are at least two people who are willing to pay different prices. Think about your own customers. Aren't there some "chef's-table" customers who you know would continue to purchase if prices were raised? Similarly, aren't there some "early-bird" shoppers who could be converted to customers if they were offered a lower price? If your company thinks about pricing primarily as an either/or, $18 or $31 type of decision, you are leaving a lot of money on the table. From this point on, pricing is not about setting numerical prices, it's about creating a set of strategies to maximize your company's profits. Just as important, these strategies are easy to create and can be implemented on Monday morning.

Anyone who sets prices can benefit from this book. That includes nonprofits (e.g., a local university alumni club), government services (e.g., public transportation), and regulated industries (e.g., local telephone services). These entities all strive to provide as much service as possible given a constraint. The constraint could be the organization's nonprofit status, fixed subsidy level, or set rate of return. No matter what, some people will value the product or service more than others will. This simple fact means that the strategies in this book are applicable to every entity that sets prices. In fact, these organizations have already started expanding the way they think about pricing beyond $18 or $31 decisions. Still dubious? Here are some examples. Older alumni, often seeking business connections, are charged more to join university alumni clubs than are freshly minted grads. Washington, D.C.'s Metro subway sets commuter prices based on time of day and distance traveled. Telephone companies charge Fortune 500 companies more for a local line connection than they do low-income customers who need a phone in case of an emergency. These organizations realize, just like Dave Straus discovered, that the right set of pricing strategies allows them to serve as many people as possible. In addition, since some customers are paying more than others, profits are increased. These new revenues can subsidize more customers or enhance services.

Hidden Profits

In today's business environment, everyone—CEOs, managers, salespeople, ambitious new hires—is under the gun to show results and grow profits. Wall Street and your boss demand a better bottom line every year, primarily from new products and new initiatives. While obviously important, these efforts are risky and costly. Most of us have a moment of doubt when we agree to meet ambitious new profit targets based on the launch of a new product or service. Pledges are made that sacrifices today will result in better profits tomorrow. Further compounding the stress is the generally long "plant-to-harvest" period before a growth investment bears profits or is written off as a bad idea.

While you must keep adding new products to avoid stagnation, what if you had a strategy that would help you hedge your bets? In addition to new products and initiatives, there are creative ways to grow by finding the hidden profits residing in your current products and services. The pricing mindset and tools in this book are the business strategy equivalent of the *Antiques Roadshow* television show. In this PBS program, the hopeful line up to have their yard-sale bargains and family heirlooms appraised. While most of the items have more sentimental than financial value, the real excitement comes when the appraiser excitedly announces that Aunt Jenny's tarnished necklace is actually a $25,000 Tiffany rarity! Families leap for joy when they discover the value that has been hidden in their attics. Your products contain a similar untapped potential to increase profits. The only difference is that in the *Antiques Roadshow,* the potential for a windfall is hit or miss. In contrast, I believe that the ability to easily increase profits exists in virtually every business product or service. A good example is the way Lloyd Hansen uncovered three billion dollars in hidden profits at Ford.

Lloyd Hansen rapidly ascended through the management ranks at Ford. After enjoying the thrill of helping turn around Ford's profit performance in Asia Pacific and other markets, he was particularly frustrated in his new position as controller of the Ford and Lincoln Mercury divisions. He felt the divisions' financial performance had stalled despite aggressive cost-cutting. As controller, he was searching for the next big thing, the idea that could boost Ford's profits and, in turn, maintain the momentum of his career. He was convinced that cost-cutting was not the entire answer. Although important, another round of cost-cutting simply would not get the job done. The anxiety of finding a new source of profit was increasingly waking him up in the middle of the night. During our interview he recalled, from the comfort of his oversized top-floor office at Ford's headquarters in Dearborn, Michigan, "It was a time of uncertainty and stress." Little did he know that Lloyd Hansen was about to discover and implement one of the most profitable business strategies in the history of Ford.

As Hansen doggedly searched for new avenues of profit, he returned to the question of whether Ford was pricing its products correctly. Intrigued, he ran an analysis of the effects on Ford's bottom line from an additional 1% of net profit margin. He could not believe the results: culling an additional penny of profit from each revenue dollar would increase Ford's net income by 33% and cash flow by 45%, and, if sustained over time, could increase Ford's market value by 45% (market value usually closely follows changes in cash flows)![1] Excited by the potential opportunity, especially in a business that is "profit-challenged," Hansen went on a mission to overhaul Ford's pricing strategy.

For many executives, pricing is the one area of their business strategy in which they feel uncomfortable and vulnerable. The problem lies in the way that they think about pricing—it's too complex. For them, pricing involves constructing a demand curve, finding the optimal price, and then managing the anxiety of wondering whether their price is indeed optimal. While Hansen shared the same apprehensions, he began wondering if there was more to pricing than just deciding what number should be listed on the invoice. Hansen embarked on broadening the view Ford took concerning pricing. Setting the actual numerical price was going to be a small, yet integral, component of his new vision of pricing.

Hansen quickly discovered that the strategies in his expanded vision of pricing yielded fabulous profits. While the strategies were straightforward, his biggest obstacle was in convincing managers handicapped by a "that's the way that we've always done it" mentality. But once they saw the results, they quickly became believers in his new pricing perspective. Hansen focused on the following four initiatives.

Empower the Sales Force. Lloyd realized that with variable profits (which account for all costs except fixed costs) ranging from less than $800 (Ford Aspire) to more than $12,000 (luxury cars like the Thunderbird), the persuasiveness of Ford's sales force could powerfully impact the company's bottom line. One of his most effective initiatives was to simply encourage and provide incentives to the sales force to sell high-margin vehicles and spend less time selling lower-margin alternatives.

Use Discounts to Up-Sell Customers.

Promotional discounts were used as an incentive for customers to trade up to more profitable bundled-model versions. For instance, in 1997 Ford's high-end SuperCab version of its Ranger pickup truck accounted for approximately 37% of all Ranger sales. Relative to a standard Ranger, an option-filled SuperCab Ranger corralled thousands more in profit. To increase the proportion of SuperCab sales, Ford knocked $700 off its price. Despite this price cut, profits soared as sales of the SuperCab increased to represent 70% of all Rangers sold.[2] Similar discounts were used to up-sell Ford Mustang customers to the model's convertible version. In addition to selling a more profitable vehicle (after accounting for the discount), Hansen found that convertible drivers also buy such high-margin options as bigger engines and leather seats.

Cross-Sell Financing. Special promotions, such as low interest rates, were offered to customers who financed their vehicles through Ford Credit. As a result of these initiatives, Ford Credit's market share of customers who opted to finance their purchase rose from 43% to 58% (a 35% increase).

Restructure Fleet Sales Mix.

The mix of sales to Ford's three primary fleet segments (government, commercial, and daily rental) was restructured. Feeling that more profits could be garnered by decreasing the number of vehicles that were sold to daily rental-car companies (like the Ford-owned Hertz), Hansen took steps to increase sales to more profitable customers. As a result, the fleet mix (1995: 58% daily rental, 31% commercial, 11% government) evolved into a more profitable mix (2000: 47% daily rental, 39% commercial, 14% government).

These four initiatives began as a one-year experiment and were rolled out in five out of Ford's eighteen sales regions. At the end of the experimental year, the regions that were doing business as usual missed their profit target by close to $300 million. The five that used the new pricing practices collectively beat their profit target by approximately $1 billion.[3] This over-the-top success led all eighteen sales regions to quickly adopt Hansen's new pricing practices in 1999. The profits quickly followed.

Hansen's focus on pricing could not have come at a better time. The global vehicle market becomes increasingly competitive with each passing year. Between 1995 and 2000, the sales volume of the Ford and Lincoln Mercury divisions increased by a mere 7%, translating into a slip in Ford's U.S. market share from 25.7% to 23.7%. Despite this lackadaisical sales growth, Ford's annual net profits skyrocketed from $3 billion to $8 billion. Ford directly attributes $3 billion of the $5 billion increase to better pricing of its vehicles.[4] Net revenue per vehicle in these years increased from $16,500 to $19,700. In

2000, the research division of the investment bank Donaldson, Lufkin & Jenrette lauded Ford's pricing efforts, stating, "The results of Ford's margin and mix program have been stunning." Hansen's focus on pricing enabled Ford to realize generous amounts of hidden profits.

Hansen moved on to other responsibilities but was recalled to the sales and marketing organization in late 2001. The weak sales environment had further degenerated because of the faltering global economy. The expensive Firestone tire recall (which created terrible negative publicity), rising product costs, and 0% financing all contributed to a lousy bottom line. Understandably, the company became distracted, and profits suffered. Hansen reinvigorated his set of road-tested pricing strategies and produced promising results. More aggressive promotions were used to up-sell customers into vehicles with higher-margin options. Ford also focused on understanding what types of pricing promotions had the best impact on its customers by collecting and analyzing data on every vehicle sale. As a result, Lloyd Hansen now knows that Explorer buyers prefer low-rate financing to cash incentives. Conversely, Focus and Crown Victoria customers prefer direct cash incentives. Ford also launched a series of new analytical tools to better match its product features and inventory with customer demand. This has proved important; 85% of Ford's vehicles are sold directly from its dealers' lots, so it's essential to have the right vehicles with the right options on each dealer's lot. These analytical tools have helped make this possible. For example, Ford used to assume that since it rarely snows in Florida, dealers there didn't need to stock many four-wheel-drive vehicles.

But after analyzing purchase data, Lloyd found strong interest in these higher-margined vehicles. Now, more four-wheel-drive vehicles are shipped to Florida, and sales are flourishing.[5] As a result of these initiatives, sales-revenue figures continue to improve. From the fourth quarter of 2001 to the end of 2004, per-vehicle revenue has increased by $2,400—an astounding amount in a competitive market. Always enthusiastic and never one to rest on his laurels, Hansen thinks that there is still more than a billion dollars in additional hidden profits that can be uncovered at Ford in the coming years.[6]

When it comes down to it, Ford did nothing unique to uncover its hidden profits. They simply understood what customers valued and priced accordingly. Any business in any industry can improve its bottom line by realizing that pricing involves far more than finding its product's "perfect price."

The State of Pricing

For most businesses, pricing is a profit-leaking paradox. Managers put a great deal of effort into making and marketing their products to create value, but where many fall short is in transforming the value they create into profits. After enduring the challenges of bringing a product to market, all too often I see critical pricing decisions being made in hastily called "pricing meetings." I recently worked with five of the smartest executives I have ever met. Their company had developed a portfolio of commercially successful video games for PlayStation, GameCube, and Xbox consoles but suddenly faced a changing marketplace as Internet-based video games became increasingly popular with game players. To serve these customers, the executives were charged with creating Web-based versions of their games. They had executed incredibly well within an extremely short time frame, but when it came time to discuss pricing, this highly capable team fell apart. Pricing their Internet games was tricky; rivals were offering free (lower-quality) and rock-bottom-priced Internet games. The executives faced the challenge that if prices for their Internet games were set too low, customers who would normally buy their high-priced console games would instead use the cheaper Internet versions. At the pricing meeting, people just started shouting out prices—$1.99 per play, $2.49 per play, two plays for $3.50—and did their best to justify their points of view. A compromise was quickly worked out, everyone scurried away, and the product's pricing was never revisited. What resulted was a price that had very little connection to the amount that consumers were willing to pay—a classic case of a product with hidden profits.

Sun Microsystems' CEO Scott McNealy recently noted that "pricing [is] confusing for us too. In the whole history of Sun, we have never known what demand is, what elasticities are, or what the 'right' prices are for our equipment."[7] If someone as sophisticated as McNealy is baffled by pricing, it is not surprising that even the smartest managers opt to simply base prices on their costs (for example, setting price on, say, three times the production cost) or on what their competitors are charging. While these convenient pricing axioms get the basic job done, they still leave ample opportunities for profit and growth on the table.

I've found that the untapped potential in pricing at most companies is similar to the unused functionality that exists in our electronic gadgets. If you're like me, there's a good chance that you are confounded by an intimidating hundred-page instruction manual. I muddle through the manual and focus on the bare minimum to get the product up and running, but leave a great deal of its functionality unused. For most companies, setting prices is a similarly frustrating experience—so many options, so many factors to incorporate, so little time and patience. What often happens is that much like how we handle the complexity of these gadgets, minimally functioning prices end up getting set. The result, of course, is hidden profits; these prices do not fully capture the amount that customers are willing to pay.

Executives at some companies are beginning to make uncovering their hidden profits a priority. For example, A. G. Lafley, Procter & Gamble's CEO, made being "priced right" one of P&G's top corporate strategic goals in 2000.[8] Many of the company's prices were changed in an effort to more accurately capture the value that customers placed on P&G products. For example, prices for Tide laundry detergent were increased by 8%, while prices for Bounty paper towels were cut by 4.5%. In a story strikingly similar to that of Ford, P&G's focus on pricing immediately paid off. In the fiscal year ending June 30, 2001, despite flat sales volume, net revenues increased by 2%. This growth was attributed in part to the company's new mix of prices. Since this initiative began, P&G has consistently cited better pricing as an integral reason for its rise in sales, profits, and stock price.

One benefit of being better at pricing is that increases generally fall directly to the bottom line. Consider a story recounted by Malcolm Gladwell in his book *The Tipping Point*: Hush Puppies shoes experienced explosive growth because the cool people in downtown Manhattan suddenly deemed them "hip." Why shouldn't the company producing Hush Puppies raise their wholesale prices by $10 to capture this newly created value? As long as demand is not tempered by the price increase, the shoe manufacturer will make $10 more in profit from every sale. There's rarely any additional cost associated with being better at pricing.

Raising your average price by a penny or two per dollar can make the difference between a good year and a great year. Since the profit margins of many companies are razor-thin, adding a few extra pennies per dollar is meaningful. A recent multi-industry analysis of profit margins found that implementing strategies that increase average prices by only one percentage point can increase operating profits (income derived from a company's own operations, thus excluding income from investments, etc.) by 11%.[9] It's surprising that Wall Street has not picked up on this tremendous upside potential. Instead of just chastising companies for not controlling their costs, Wall Street should be hammering companies that are not more masterful with their pricing.

Pricing Is More Than a Number; It's a Series of Integrated Strategies

Conventional wisdom in business often views pricing as the search for that one "perfect price"—the nirvana where profits are maximized—for their product or service. However, making pricing decisions on this basis inevitably results in a catch-22. If you price too high, sales are lost from potential customers who are not willing to pay that much (but who *would* pay less). On the other hand, price too low and you'll miss profits from those who are willing to pay more. The problems with this approach are twofold. First, it's hard to find the perfect price. The difficulty of this challenge often causes managers to give up and settle on a price that "just works." But the real problem is that this approach to pricing absolutely guarantees that your product will have hidden profits.

Trying to find a product's optimal price point is never easy. Should it, like Dave Straus's question about pricing items on his menu, be $18 or $31? A good starting point involves using market research to gain insights into the amount that customers are willing to pay for your product. But before commissioning a study, it's important to understand the role that market research should play in setting price. First, market research is not a black box that can somehow calculate your product's optimal price. In addition, there is often a time lag between when a pricing study is done and when its recommendations are implemented. If market conditions change during this time period, as they sometimes do, this usually results in a new optimal price. That said, with these perspectives in mind, in my experience the insights gained from market research are invaluable in helping managers and their team set prices.

Even if you can find this mythical perfect price, your product will be loaded with hidden profits. Think about all the profits (from the chef's table) and growth (from early-bird specials) you'll miss out on if the scope of your pricing is limited to pricing catch-22 types of $18 or $31 decisions. So, when making your pricing decisions, don't fall victim to the forest-for-the-trees syndrome. There are several other options besides a potentially brand-damaging unilateral price increase that can help you achieve a few percentage points of increased profit margin. While the amount that customers pay is certainly important, pricing can do so much more.

Though simple, the concept of different customers having different valuations (and, therefore, different prices that they are willing to pay) for the same product is based on one of the most important building blocks in economic analysis: the law of demand. Most of us believe (and have experienced) the key point of the law of demand: a lower price will attract more customers. New customers attracted by a lower price are always interested in the product, just not at the higher price that others willingly pay.

Think about the most treasured item you own. How much would your friends pay for the same product? A quick survey will undoubtedly reveal a broad range of prices. Even very similar people will value products differently. Haven't you ever been surprised at how your friends spend their money? Mine certainly were when I paid $5,000 for a lime-green couch.

I could tell by their expressions that they were thinking, "How could a guy normally so cool buy something like *that*?" (No matter what they think, I still believe that couch is hip.) The amount that customers are willing to pay is subjective, and understanding that is the key to successful pricing.

This subjective nature of pricing creates the pricing catch-22. You face a sea of customers, and each is willing to pay a different price. The difference between the lowest and highest valuations can be significant. The multi-price mindset, a central idea I will develop throughout this book, shows how to view pricing as a series of strategies that allow you to serve the broadest range of customers and reap different profit margins (small to large) based on the values purchasers place on the product—for example, through early-bird and chef's-table strategies.

Several industries selling perishable goods have already adopted some form of the multi-price mindset. For example, airlines offer first-class seating and a bevy of prices based on whether you meet the right restrictions (advance purchase, minimum stay, senior discounts, etc.). American Airlines even sold unlimited lifetime first-class-travel air passes to individuals for $250,000 in the 1980s! Similarly, your local movie theater offers discounted matinee tickets, and cinemas like the Loews Cineplex on 34th Street in Manhattan charge a $5 premium for reserved seating in posh leather chairs. So why haven't other industries done likewise? My feeling is that the pain of watching profits vanish on a daily basis (because their products perish) has motivated these industries to proactively use price to recover their hidden profits. What all businesses need to understand is that the profits lost from *not* offering chef's-table and early-bird strategies are exactly analogous to those lost when an airplane takes off half-full.

The beauty of the ideas in this book is that they can be formulated into strategies that can be implemented on Monday morning. Here's what seems like an obvious example. Consider Bruce Springsteen's wildly successful concert tour to support his CD *The Rising*. At the majority of his concerts, all tickets were priced at $75. The best seats in the house cost the same as the worst. The price was the same regardless of how popular Springsteen was in any particular city. A survey of 858 concertgoers in Philadelphia, a city where tickets to Mr. Springsteen's concert quickly sold out, found that 27% had purchased tickets from scalpers at an average price of $280 a ticket.[10] Conversely, sales were so lackluster for his concert at the eighty-thousand-seat Ralph Wilson Stadium in Buffalo that it had to be moved to the nearby twenty-thousand-seat Darien Lake Performing Arts Center.[11] Had "The Boss" been so inclined, a few simple strokes of the pricing pen could have instantly enhanced his profits. Obvious changes include increasing prices in high-demand regions and for prime seats, as well as decreasing prices in cities where he is less popular. Pretty straightforward, right? My bet is that after you read this book, you too will be able to make changes that are easy to envision and implement. These small tweaks will result in immediate profit boosts.

Is Being Adept at Pricing a Bad Thing?

When I tell my friends that I am writing a book on pricing, many smirk and flippantly retort, "Oh, ripping off the consumer." Others seem to feel guilty about pricing. So, it's a good question: Is being adept at pricing a bad thing?

There are few things more satisfying than watching an entrepreneur who endured the hardships that came with making her vision a reality experience the thrill of gaining consumer acceptance. Entrepreneurship—bringing something new to the market—is the foundation of our economy and the nucleus of growth. Consumers win because of the many product choices available and the constant flow of inventions that make life easier and more interesting. I've sweated through this entrepreneurial jungle myself, with the eighty-hour workweeks, the financial risks, the obstacles to be overcome, and the resulting successes and failures. Entrepreneurs are entitled to profit. And profit, which is directly linked to pricing, is the carrot that drives our entrepreneurial system.

Since most products are not essential to life, consumers always have the right to say no to high prices. I recently considered buying a Toyota Prius hybrid car. In part because of its adoption by many Hollywood movie stars, the Prius has become an affordable "status" car. Going from dealer to dealer, I found that the story was the same: instant sellouts, waiting lists, and the discouraging phrase, "It's going for about forty-five hundred dollars above the list price." In the end, I decided that the price was too high *for me*. Despite the loss of my purchase, the Prius is selling well. Toyota and its dealers are making money, the environment is being saved, and many drivers are commuting in style. I'll eventually get my hybrid car—when prices drop. My point is that no one should feel sorry for me because I opted not to be the first person on my block to own a Prius. It's all about choice and personal decisions regarding what's important to me and how I spend my money.

The multi-price mindset also benefits customers. Firms are encouraged to price in a manner that allows more customers to enjoy their product as well as provides opportunities to enhance customer satisfaction. As Dave Straus (the restaurateur) realized, the set of pricing strategies allows more people to enjoy his restaurant than if he were simply pricing entrées at $24.50. The multi-price mindset also encourages firms to offer a menu of purchasing options, with some items providing more profit than others. The fact that some Ritz-Carlton customers opt to stay in higher-margin luxury suites really translates into these customers saying, "Even accounting for the higher prices, I enjoy staying in suites more than regular rooms." (Or, of course, they may be spending someone else's money while on an expense account.)

A well-planned pricing strategy generally does not result in a net loss to society, either. Even if some customers end up paying more, this leads to higher profits. If your company makes more money from a better pricing strategy, hopefully this will result in more money in your wallet through a raise or a "we had a good year" bonus. Enhanced profits also increase the stock price of a company. Many of us are counting on our

401(k) portfolios to fund our retirement. Who wouldn't appreciate the security brought on by a rise in their portfolio's value? In fact, stockholders should be upset if their management has not adopted a multi-price mindset. So, yes, companies will make more money from a good pricing strategy, but these profits don't go into a vacuum. Your next-door neighbors (company employees and shareholders) also benefit from pricing for profits and growth.

Finally, companies may not have a choice. If rivals are better at pricing, companies risk losing customers and eventually end up competing against firms that are better capitalized because they price for profits and growth. For example, after years of watching Lloyd Hansen's pricing success at Ford, both General Motors and DaimlerChrysler made similar efforts to better manage their pricing. Mastering the strategy of pricing is essential to prospering in our increasingly competitive business environment.

Overview

Thematically, this book is divided into two primary sections. Chapters 2 through 4 comprise the "new ideas" section of the book. This section provides the building blocks of the pricing for profits and growth philosophy. Chapter 2 discusses the importance of creating a business environment that allows you to profit from better pricing. Chapter 3 highlights the central role value plays in setting prices. Chapter 4 introduces Lessons from an Auction, the concept of different customers having different valuations for the same product. This anomaly is what expands the scope of pricing beyond simply finding the right invoice price into a powerful set of strategies.

Once you've adopted these perspectives, you'll find a wealth of opportunities to uncover your product's hidden profits. The second section, chapters 5 through 9, provides a comprehensive set of strategies that will enable you to price for profits and growth. Chapter 5 presents a framework, the Value Decoder, to help you understand the value of your product. Differential pricing, the strategy of charging different prices to different customers, is presented in Chapter 6. Chapter 7 discusses versioning, the strategy of offering customers a line of products with different prices (e.g., good, better, best) and allowing them to select the one that best fits their valuation. Chapter 8 shows how offering new pricing strategies can activate dormant customers, those who are interested in your product but haven't purchased because your pricing method (e.g., individual sales, leasing, bundling, etc.) doesn't appeal to them. The strategy section wraps up in Chapter 9 with a discussion of the conditions (e.g., strategic, fairness) in which you may want to lower your prices and psychological strategies that can make your price more appealing to customers. Chapter 10 sums up all of the concepts discussed in this book.

CHAPTER 2

The Culture of Profit

The Culture of Profit

I recently had the good fortune to discuss pricing with Ron Tadross, the respected Bank of America auto-investment analyst. It was a fascinating conversation that ended up focusing on two Fortune 500 companies operating in the same industry. Both have lean cost structures, good management, and sell popular products. But that's where the similarities end. The smaller company's profits are almost double that of its rival's. "How can this be?" I asked in amazement. Ron coolly responded, "One has a culture of profit and the other doesn't."[12]

A culture of profit is a business environment and shared way of thinking that allows your company to price for profits and growth. Think of this as the prep work that lays the foundation so that your business will benefit from an effective pricing strategy. You may ask: "Rafi, why do I need to create a *culture*? Can't the people on my staff that set prices just read your book?" Unfortunately, it's not that easy. The reason you have to create a company-wide culture is because so many people in your organization touch pricing. Marketing sets prices and runs discount promotions; the sales force usually has the power to negotiate prices; the distribution department affects price by matching supply and demand in individual regions (too much supply results in lower prices, and shortages increase prices); finance's promotional payment plans (e.g., 0% financing) ultimately affect the net price; and managers often have the authority to change prices at will. Given that so many people influence pricing, everyone needs to understand how their actions affect price. Everyone has to have the right incentives, information, and tools for your company to price for profits and growth.

Let me show you how to create a culture of profit.

Basic Information + Small Changes = Large Benefits

Like many of you who are pushing hard to pursue your dreams, the last few years have been a struggle for me. I've been pulled in many different directions, some good and some bad. One consequence of this building period was that my health suffered. I recently decided to focus on getting back into shape and within six months lost thirty-five pounds. Perhaps thinking about the topic of my next book, my literary agent demanded to know my "secret." I could feel the disappointment when I replied, "Simply exercising and eating smarter." Regrettably, I have not invented a revolutionary potato-chip, fast-food, and no-exercise diet. The lesson I learned is simply the mantra of weight-loss experts: "Change your lifestyle."

What's interesting about my experience is that I did not *radically* change my lifestyle. In retrospect, all the things I did were obvious. First, I became more knowledgeable about the foods I ate. For instance, I never realized that my morning blueberry muffin, which I used to think was healthy, contained more calories than a Fatburger from the West Coast–based Fatburger hamburger chain, nor did I understand that I could save 120 calories by cooking my eggs with Pam vegetable spray instead of margarine. Armed with this new knowledge, I implemented small changes and made becoming healthier a priority in my life. I soon discovered that these obvious changes had powerful effects on *my* bottom line.

My experience of getting back into shape mirrors the process that companies can use to create a culture of profit. It's about providing information and making small changes. Providing the right information to your employees allows them to do their jobs in a more profitable manner. Similarly, a few obvious changes can make your company more money. Creating a culture of profit will have two powerful effects. First, many of these changes are straightforward to implement and can quickly start generating new profits. Second, and more important, this culture enables your business to grow. It's not a one-shot deal. Returning to my weight-loss analogy, we all have experienced or know people whose weight has yo-yoed. We work very hard, get into a slump, and then get back on the treadmill. As I realized, weight loss is about changing my lifestyle, consistently eating well and exercising regularly. Similarly, a culture of profit changes your company's lifestyle. It creates a sustainable competitive advantage that enables your company to profit and grow.

Empower Your Employees to Make You More Money

Not long ago, the *Wall Street Journal*'s Cranky Consumer wrote about his experience of phoning pizza-delivery chains and simply asking for a discount.[13] Interestingly, four out of five phone clerks responded with a lower price or better deal. One Papa John's employee took 30% off the price of two pizzas and allowed the Cranky Consumer to talk an additional $2.50 off an order of chicken strips. Not to be outdone, a Pizza Hut employee offered a special $19.99 deal for two pizzas and chicken wings, a 48% discount off regular prices. Given that the food-service consulting firm Technomic estimates that the average profit on a $9 pizza is $2, these profit-draining discounts are significant.

I recently benefited from a similar experience. Shopping at

a department store near my home, I brought $200 worth of merchandise to the cash register. The amiable young clerk smiled and mentioned that there was a coupon in the newspaper for 15% off all items in her department. Luckily, she had an extra coupon, so she scanned it into the register and I saved $30. Not only was I delighted, I could tell that she felt good about helping me save money. The only one who did not share our brief moment of happiness was her employer, the department store. Unaware of the coupon (and believe me, it's rare that I would miss out on such a discount), I had approached the cash register fully intending to pay $200. The clerk's generosity chopped $30 directly off the department store's profit margin.

Most companies do not realize the power that their front line (employees who directly interact with customers) has on profits. I doubt that these pizza and department-store clerks understood how their generous gestures affected their employers' bottom line. It's natural to want to make people happy, and really, who doesn't enjoy a good discount? Employees are not doing anything illegal or unethical; they are just trying to be nice. But even something as innocuous as a well-intentioned whisper to "come back tomorrow because the products in your hand will be on sale" results in lost profits. There are many other ways that your employees can profitably enhance a customer's experience. For example, going the extra mile to assist customers usually results in the same shared happiness produced by an unexpected discount, as well as engendering loyalty—"they always take good care of me." In fact, many businesses make customer satisfaction, measured by monthly surveys, a key criterion for promotion. While you always want satisfied customers, it is also your responsibility to make sure that your employees understand how their actions affect the bottom line of the business.

Share Information. The first step to empowering employees is to share information on product profitability. For most companies, some products make more money than others do. Your sales force has the ability to steer customers toward higher-margined products. How many times have you been swayed by a salesclerk's recommendation? It also goes beyond the power of persuasion; your sales force should be investing its time on your most profitable customers and products. Don't waste this lucrative opportunity; your sales force will make you more money when they are fully informed and not in the dark.

For example, the effect on Ford's profits of sharing product and customer information is nothing short of astounding. At a 1995 sales-team meeting held at the Ann Arbor, Michigan, Marriott, Ford took the unprecedented step of distributing its highly guarded yellow card to its sales team. This card detailed the variable profit on each of Ford's vehicles. Prior to that point, only members of the finance team had access to this information. Thus, the sales force had operated with no idea which vehicles and options were the most profitable. As he was describing this pivotal meeting to me, Lloyd Hansen paused to gaze out the window. It had been an emotional event. Withholding this information had long been a sore spot for the sales force; they viewed this secretiveness as a sign of distrust. Once the yellow card was finally shared, there was an overwhelming outpouring of emotion and joy. Sharing this sensitive information made the sales force feel like partners with the company, instead of laborers pushing volume. They relished the feeling of trust and their newly created ability to make Ford more money.

The energized sales force began concentrating on making sales that were in both Ford's and its customers' best interests. One surprising revelation, as discussed in Chapter 1, was how widely the variable profits differed between the vehicles in Ford's product line. For example, Mustangs were ten times more profitable than Probes. No one had imagined that the difference was so great. Prior to sharing the yellow card, the sales organization was spending a disproportionate amount of time selling Probes, which were much more difficult to sell than Mustangs. Sales of the Mustang were so slow that its production line was shut down one week per month. Armed with the new information, the sales force changed their focus to the Mustang—including highlighting the muscle car's key attributes to upgrade customers into this higher-margin vehicle. As a result, shortly after the meeting, production of the Probe dropped, while the Mustang's production raced to maximum overtime. This information allowed everyone to focus on the same goal: making Ford more money.

How much is your sales force in the dark about the profitability of your product line? How much more money could you make by sharing profit information with them?

An additional effect of sharing profit information is showing employees how healthy or thin your net profits are. Many people don't understand what profit is; some think of it as revenue, or confuse gross profit (revenue minus cost of goods sold) with net profit (a company's earnings, reflecting revenues adjusted for costs of doing business, depreciation, interest, taxes, and other expenses). This information hammers home the message that what they are doing every day has a significant effect on the bottom line. This kind of transparency has the potential to increase morale, since everyone knows they can make a difference in terms of how they do their work.

When profit margins are thin, minor tweaks in price can dramatically affect profits and market values. Table 2-1 shows the total revenues, net profits, and profit margins of several well-known Fortune 25 companies. Net profits are typically a few percentage points gleaned off a large volume of revenue. Recall Lloyd Hansen's analysis that a 1% increase in price that flowed directly to the bottom line would translate into a 33% increase in net profit. For most companies, increasing price by one percent (tacking on one penny to each dollar of a product's price) can have an astounding effect on net profits.

One percent, such a small number, can usually be achieved within a large organization. Everyone needs to realize that a few dollars either way on price can mean the difference between a generous raise and rumors of cost-cutting. For example, if everyone at Kroger concentrated on increasing prices by just 1% (a $100 grocery bill would become $101), the company's net profits would almost triple. What would an additional percentage of profit (garnered from a price increase) do to your company's net profit and market value? Could a little extra vigilance on promotions and a more determined focus on price result in an additional point of net profit? For most of us, the answer is yes.

	Revenues Millions	Net Profits Millions	Profit Margin
Table 2-1 Profit Margins of Select Fortune 25 Companies			
Wal-Mart	258,681.0	9,054.0	3.5%
ExxonMobil	213,199.0	21,510.0	10.09%
General Motors	195,645.2	3,822.0	1.95%
General Electric	134,187.0	15,002.0	11.18%
Citigroup	94,713.0	17,853.0	18.85%
Hewlett-Packard	73,061.0	2,539.0	3.48%
Cardinal Health	56,829.5	1,405.8	2.47%
State Farm Insurance	56,064.6	2,825.9	5.04%
Kroger	53,790.8	314.6	0.58%
Boeing	50,485.0	698.0	1.38%

* From *Fortune* magazine's 2004 Fortune 500 list

As mentioned in Chapter 1, a recent study of the Global 1200 (twelve hundred large, publicly traded companies from around the world) found that for these companies, a net price increase of 1% would on average result in an 11% increase in operating profits.[14] Let me clarify a few terms in this statement: (a) by net price increase, I mean the price increase does not affect the quantity of products sold, and (b) operating profits are the income derived from a company's own operations (excluding other incomes, such as those gained from financial investments). Suppose this 1% to 11% ratio applies to my book publisher, and the wholesale price of this book is $10. If my publisher achieved a 1% net price increase (e.g., the wholesale price rises by ten cents, and this is carried through, so the retail price goes from $24.95 to $25.05), its operating profits would rise by 11%. Similarly, if wholesale prices were raised by 10% (e.g., resulting in this book's retail price increasing to $25.95), its operating profits would jump by 110%. Now that's eye-opening! Of course, the potential downside of raising prices is that demand will decrease. Let me ask you, would a $1 increase in this book's price have stopped you from buying it? This is the type of question you should be asking about your products. Will a 1% price increase really cause your customers to stop purchasing from you?

Provide Guidelines to Cut Prices. Many of your employees are entrusted with the power to offer lower prices. The key question is *when* should prices be dropped? Sure, offering a reduced price to your best friend's cousin is nice, but it's rarely the most profitable use of a discount. An employee's discretionary pricing powers are typically best used in the following three situations. Discounts can be used to *upsell* customers to a more profitable product. Why not offer a customer who has decided to buy a laser printer a good deal to trade up to a more profitable (after accounting for the discount) color printer? Experienced salespeople also use discounts in their *negotiations* with customers. Their goal is to find the right price that will make customers say yes. Finally, a common use of discretionary discounts is to *win sales away from competitors*.

In competitive situations, you have to understand how

your product differs from the competition's. If the Home Depot next door is offering a lower price on the same product you're selling, it's probably reasonable to match their price. That said, products rarely offer identical value. Sellers willing to negotiate on price need to understand and capture their product's unique value. As a cash-challenged graduate student in upstate New York, I used to show up at local retailers asking that they match the prices advertised in *The Village Voice* by Manhattan electronics stores (located 250 miles away). In retrospect, it is surprising how many local merchants willingly matched those rock-bottom prices. Only one retailer had the right reaction; his response to my bold request was, "There is something of value, something that you cannot get from this *Village Voice* advertiser, that led you to my store. So I am not willing to match the price." This response was right on the mark. What did I value? I valued getting the product immediately and dealing with a local firm if I had problems. My point here is this: in match-the-competition's-price scenarios, your front line needs to highlight and fight to monetize your product's unique value.

To help make these profit-critical decisions, your company should provide the following guidelines on cutting prices:

Rule 1: How low should a price go? Sometimes (e.g., when matching competitors) it makes sense to offer a price that is below your average cost (takes into account all costs, such as salaries, rent, production costs, etc.). One point of caution: your employees need to understand that everyone cannot receive a price that is below average cost. To stay in business, your *average price* (the average, weighted by volume, of your mix of high through low prices) needs to be greater than your average cost. However, prices should not drop below your product's incremental (production or wholesale) cost. For example, prices at a kids' lemonade stand should never be lower than their production (lemons, sugar, and associated labor to make the drink) or wholesale (in the event that they are selling cans of lemonade, the price that they paid for each can) costs. It's rarely profitable to sell products at prices that are below your actual cost (although retailers often offer loss-leader products in the hope that customers will also purchase higher-margined products).

Rule 2:   The price cut should be targeted and discrete. If other customers find out about the discount, your phone will soon be ringing with demands for similar reductions. If this occurs, a quick discount to make a sale will turn into a very expensive mistake.

Rule 3:   Make sure that discounted sales do not block purchases from those who are willing to pay full price. Selling a $10-a-day upgrade to the last convertible on the car-rental lot is fine, unless the next customer in line is willing to pay $50 more per day for the opportunity to drive with the top down.

Create Confidence in Your Product. Because your employees interact with customers and potential customers, they have to be confident about your product's value. Everyone needs to understand and feel good about the

value your products offer. This confidence allows your employees to look customers straight in the eye and assuredly convey that even at the current price, they are getting a great deal.

One of my favorite restaurants in Boston is Uncle Pete's Hickory Ribs. Personally, I think it's the mixture of hickory, oak, and apple wood smoke that Pete uses in his "secret" three-day barbecue process that makes his ribs the best I've ever tasted. After a recent dinner at Pete's, I started thinking about how lucky I was that he and his wonderful wife, Pha, had opened this restaurant. As we were saying our customary good-byes and thank-yous, I took a moment to share the feelings that make me return to the restaurant and recommend it to friends: "I really should be thanking you for opening such a great restaurant. I love coming here." While the common convention is that sellers should be grateful to their customers, it's important to remember that transactions are two-way streets. The point that I am trying to make is that when customers purchase your product, they are in essence saying, "Thank you, your product offered me the best value among all of your competitors."

This is not arrogance or lack of appreciation for customers, just a reminder that you provide customers with a valuable product or service. I know a lot of smart managers who lose sight of the value they provide and end up being bullied by their customers on price. It helps for you to consistently think of the value you provide your customers. If you can't confidently articulate the value you provide, do you think that your customers fully understand the value they are receiving? For example, consider Boeing's insistence on pricing its aircraft at a premium relative to those of its rival, Airbus. The problem is that Boeing is not doing a good job of justifying its premium to customers. For instance, their planes offer more value than Airbus's because they are lighter. This results in long-term cost savings from better fuel efficiency. But Boeing's inability to clearly justify their jetliners' value has resulted in a string of order losses to Airbus.[15]

You should not hesitate to charge what you think your product is worth. I often hear social commentators opine that corporations should share their products' value with customers (i.e., lower their prices). I disagree. I think that you are entitled to fully profit from your entrepreneurial efforts. Is the capitalist who sells a product for $50 to consumers who value the product at $100 a nice guy or a stupid businessman? How would you feel if you held this share-the-value businessman's stock in your 401(k) plan? Keep your focus on maximizing profits. Your shareholders always have the option to contribute to their favorite charities with *their* profits.

Another faulty idea is the notion of *goodwill*, one of the most overrated words in pricing. Managers often try to justify questionable price cuts with the belief that discounts will develop goodwill and foster relationships. Seriously, if a competitor's product offers better quality at a lower price, how many "relationship" customers will stay with something that has lower quality at a higher price? The harsh truth is that most customers will continue purchasing only as long as your product provides the best value for their dollar. Ask the long list of failed Mom & Pop stores how much their hallowed small-town customer relationships mattered once Wal-Mart moved to town. Creating goodwill may make you feel better, but it doesn't ensure customer loyalty.

Instead of offering goodwill discounts, think of your best customers as prime targets for collecting additional profits. If customers value your product highly, they will often be willing to pay you more money. You just have to give them the opportunity. For instance, *offering different quality levels* allows companies to further profit from loyal customers. Johnnie Walker uses this strategy by offering different labeled (red = good, black = better, gold = best, and blue = very best) versions of its scotch whisky. Most customers purchase its red- ($26) or black-label ($35) scotch. However, the gold- ($85) and blue- ($200) labeled premium versions reap higher margins from the company's most loyal customers. Similarly, many businesses offer a path of products to *bring customers into the family* and eventually upgrade profits from loyal customers. For example, both Mercedes-Benz and BMW offer "starter" models targeted toward younger, less affluent customers. The hope is that as these customers' incomes increase, they will trade up to more expensive models. Finally, additional products can be *cross-sold* to your customers. Alpine Valley Water, a leading water-cooler and bottled-water company in Cincinnati, now collects more profits from its customers by selling additional products such as coffee and twenty-two-ounce sports bottles of water.

As noted earlier, Ford has done a good job of upgrading its loyal customers into more luxurious (and profitable) vehicles. Once the yellow card was shared, the sales force learned that the Grand Marquis was one of Ford's most profitable models. Yet due to slow sales, its production line was shut down one week per month. After discovering its high margins, sales representatives in the fleet division worked to upgrade their loyal accounts into the Grand Marquis. Car-rental companies (Hertz, Budget, and Enterprise) were successfully sold on the notion that their customers would pay more for the luxury of driving a Grand Marquis. One success involved converting an Enterprise Rent-A-Car order of twenty thousand low-margin Aspires into a substantially more profitable order for twenty thousand Grand Marquises. The confidence of conveying its enhanced value drove production of the Grand Marquis to maximum overtime.[16]

Plug the Leaks in
Your Pricing Practices

Now is a good time to reevaluate your pricing and promotional policies to see if they are conducive to a culture of profit. Are the right customers taking advantage of your discounted prices and promotions? Are there flawed policies that you should withdraw? My bet is that in this examination, you'll find ways to plug some leaks in your profit flow.

Close the Back Door to Unnecessary Discounts. My sister, a researcher at a Midwestern university, recently called to seek my help in renting a minivan for eight days. She and her family planned to drive to Florida during the university's upcoming spring break. I was delighted to help, as I gain pleasure in finding a good car-rental rate—it's like cracking the code of a safe! Whenever I call a car-rental company, I list every possible discount I am eligible for (e.g., membership to AAA, coupons I received in the mail, promotional codes listed in the newspaper, etc.). And what's so fascinating is that there is usually a different rate for every discount I mention. I pity the reservations agent who answers my call. Inevitably, after going through my laundry list of discounts, I hit the jackpot and get a great rate.

On this particular occasion, I wasn't doing very well. After listing all the possible discounts that my sister qualified for, the lowest quoted price was $407 for eight days. Disgruntled, I hung up, but then immediately called back. After listing the same discounts, the safe cracked; the rate dropped to $268 if my sister could show a valid university identification card. My joy was tempered when the agent added the caveat that this rate provided eight hundred free miles and charged twenty-five cents for every mile above that limit. Given that the trip to Florida is eleven hundred miles one-way, this deal was of no use to my sister. When I mentioned my need for unlimited mileage, much to my surprise, I was told that the same rate *with* unlimited mileage was also available (Ding! Ding! Ding!). The story does not end here. The car-rental company had a promotion on their website offering one free day if you signed up for their frequent-renter program. Thus, the price dropped further, to $226. There probably is a good reason for offering discounts to faculty members, but perhaps the spring-break dates should be blacked out and a higher price should be charged for the option of unlimited mileage. Additionally, I am not sure why the price dropped so much between phone calls, but this glitch (either computer or employee) also needs to be remedied.

What backdoor discounts do you need to fix?

Fix Unprofitable Promotions. David Phillips will forever be known as "the pudding guy." The unassuming California civil engineer found a huge leak in a promotion being run for Healthy Choice products. This maker of nutritious food products was running a promotion offering a thousand frequent-flier miles for every ten Universal Product Codes (UPC) from its products. After finding cups of chocolate pudding selling for twenty-five cents apiece, Mr. Phillips became focused on making the most of the promotion. After spending $3,140 on Healthy Choice products (including 12,150 cups of pudding), he was rewarded with 1.25 million frequent-flier miles (good for fifty round-trips in the United States). Given that airlines typically sell frequent-flier miles for two cents a mile, Mr. Phillips's fortitude cost Healthy Choice approximately $25,000.[17]

And David Phillips was no one-hit wonder. One year later, he struck again. Preying on a promotion run by LatinPass, a consortium of Latin American airlines, he spent two weekends traveling on thirteen different airlines. What would possess someone to spend $2,500 to fly on so many airlines in such a short time? A promotional bonus of another one million frequent-flier miles on American Airlines![18]

Hopefully your promotions don't have these types of leaks. However, it's not unusual for resourceful customers to figure out how to make the most out of promotions. For example, posters on the website FatWallet.com often list loss-leader merchandise and strategies to exploit loopholes in rebate offers. Are the right customers taking advantage of your promotions?

Reward the Right Customers. Many companies lavish their best customers with expensive amenities and services. That's fine, but it's important that the *right* customers benefit from these premiums. For example, most airlines offer several levels of elite status to their best customers. Elite status generally confers such benefits as first-class upgrades, early boarding, and better customer service. To start enjoying these benefits, most airlines require that you fly twenty-five thousand miles a year. Thus, transcontinental fliers can earn elite status by making as few as five round-trips. Enduring twenty-five thousand miles on a plane is not the best indicator of whether a customer is profitable. There is a large difference in profitability between full-fare (paying $2,400 round-trip) and low-fare (often paying as little as $200 round-trip) cross-country travelers. Now think about your customer base. Are you giving away value at the expense of both your profits and the patience of your high-margin customers? How much hidden profit could be recovered from a review of your complimentary services and clients being pampered with specialized attention?

Use the Right Metrics of Success. To maximize your product's profits, your metrics of success have to focus on profitability. I know that many of you are probably thinking, "Thanks for stating the obvious, Rafi." Well, in my

experience, the metrics that most companies use to gauge success rarely measure profitability.

Some companies allocate a fixed marketing-costs budget to each member of their sales team (or reward those who keep their marketing costs low). By marketing costs, I mean a total dollar figure that can be discounted off the list prices of all their sales (e.g., $20,000 in list-price discounts per month). The sales force typically has complete discretion over how they use their budget. The problem is that all dollar discounts are not equal, both in terms of improving the likelihood of a sale and, more important, in how they affect a company's bottom line. For example, a $1,000 discount on an entry-level product (e.g., a $15,000 basic tractor) is more likely to generate a sale compared to using the same $1,000 discount to reduce the price of a high-end product (e.g., a $50,000 tractor loaded with amenities). So what often happens is that marketing-cost budgets get squandered on selling relatively low-priced products with thin margins. Marketing-cost budgets also fail to take into account the fact that in terms of a company's profitability, a $1,000 discount on a $15,000 entry product may be equivalent to reducing a top-of-the-line $50,000 product by $8,000. One simple alternative is to instead reward salespeople based on the total profits generated by their sales.

Similarly, many companies view an agreed-upon invoice price as indicative of a transaction's profitability. An invoice price of $6 a unit sounds better than an invoice price of $5 per unit. But in business, as in life, it's the little things that matter. To understand the profitability of a transaction, off-invoice discounts (e.g., volume, cash payment, or corporate affiliation) have to be taken into account. While these discounts may not amount to much individually, the aggregate sum can be significant. After factoring in these types of discounts, it's possible for a $5 invoice price to be more profitable than an off-invoice, discount-laden $6 price.

It's always revealing to undertake what I call a naked price audit of a company's accounts. For each account, this analysis subtracts all the discounts from the agreed-upon invoice price to determine the naked net price. Once these discounts are stripped away, managers are often surprised to see the wide variation of net prices paid by their customers. A recent study found a 500% difference between the lowest and highest naked net prices for a fastener supplier.[19] This exercise motivates managers to be more restrained in handing out off-invoice discounts. Inevitably, this audit will reveal that some customers have been able to take advantage of greater discounts then they really should be receiving. These accounts can be brought into line by increasing prices. Just as important, lucrative customers who are not immediately recognizable by their invoice prices can begin to receive better sales attention.

Of course, net prices shouldn't necessarily be the same for each account. Account-specific discounts can be justified by such factors as volume considerations, local competition, or geographic economic conditions. It is important to note that some customers may receive low prices simply because they are unable to pay more. It's usually in your best interest to offer a wide range of net prices. Remember what I said before: *on average*, prices have to be greater than average costs. Just make sure that the right customers are paying the right prices.[20]

It is also necessary to evaluate whether you are using the right metrics to measure your company's success. Most companies focus on achieving the highest possible market share. Unfortunately, achieving the largest market share in a competitive market is rarely the most profitable operating point for a company. The drawback of focusing on market share is that often prices have to be lowered to attract more customers. You don't want to end up in a situation in which you are selling a lot of volume but, because prices had to be dropped, not making much money off of each customer. In their race to boast "I am bigger," many managers do not realize that pursuing this trophy comes at the expense of their bottom line. There is usually a trade-off between customer profitability and market share. The compromise is to focus on profitable volume. This metric focuses on reaching the market share point where total profits (volume multiplied by customer profitability) are maximized. For most companies, profitable volume is the right gauge to measure sales success.

Several years ago, Lloyd Hansen decided to use profitable volume as the metric for Ford's sales success. Prior to this decision, it was not uncommon for Ron Robbins, Ford's point man for selling more than one million new fleet cars as well as an additional million used cars per year, to receive instructions from corporate headquarters to promptly unload forty thousand Tempos or twenty thousand Tauruses.[21] Executing these orders invariably led to setting rock-bottom prices, which in turn lowered the resale values of leased vehicles that the company eventually had to take back. To remedy the ills of focusing on volume and market share, Ron instructed his fleet sales force to treat each account as a business unit of one. The mandate was to make each business unit profitable. While difficult at times, the sales team began walking away from long-standing relationship deals if profit margins dropped too low. Focusing on profitable volume yielded spectacular results—Ron Robbins's division went from being a nonprofit, low-margin division to a $1 billion a year profit center.

It's also important to understand how the sales-force quotas that companies pursuing market share usually impose can affect profitability. Thrifty customers—those who are less time-sensitive and more forward-thinking—often eagerly await the predictable end-of-the-quarter fire-sale call from their salesperson. In their sprint to meet quotas, salespeople typically offer terrific deals. How many of your customers play this game of waiting out the margin? Would these customers have purchased at full price had this option not been available? How many points of net profit is the quota game of waiting out the margin costing your shareholders?

Configure Your Organization to Price

Hopefully, you're now convinced that the actions of many different parts of your organization affect your prices. Given the importance of pricing, it makes sense to coordinate the activities of these various departments. Many companies are creating councils, comprised of the leadership of departments that influence pricing, to implement cohesive pricing strategies.[22]

Bill Ford, Ford's chief executive officer, created a revenue-management organization to further improve pricing in the fourth quarter of 2001. This new organization was an integral part of the company's revitalization plan. One of its primary responsibilities was to coordinate and use new technology to manage all of Ford's key pricing activities—including marketing incentives, production programming, and distribution of vehicles. This structure allowed Ford to continue to increase the net revenue realized on each sale. And who did Bill Ford choose to promote to run this department and become a company officer? Our good friend Lloyd Hansen, who led the initiative to have Ford develop a pricing strategy based on transparency and the value offered to customers.

CHAPTER 3

It's All About Value

The Fluctuating Value of an Umbrella

Washington, D.C., is one of my favorite cities. Its historic monuments, museums, and cosmopolitan culture make it a wonderful place to visit. No trip there is complete without visiting the National Mall area, a 2.5-mile, tree-lined grassy strip containing many of Washington's most famous attractions, including the Lincoln Memorial, Washington Monument, Smithsonian Museums, and Capitol Building. Amid this beauty and historic splendor, enterprising street vendors sell everything from bottled water to T-shirts announcing MY PARENTS VISITED THE NATION'S CAPITAL AND ALL I GOT WAS THIS LOUSY SHIRT. Of course, Washington is by no means unique with all of these—I know, for instance, that Hawaii and New York also have those shirts (thanks, Mom and Dad).

Taste notwithstanding, these vendors set prices in a way that every company needs to understand and incorporate into its business practice. These savvy sellers understand that customers base the price they are willing to pay on the value they receive from a product. So, at the first hint of rain, street vendors double the price of their umbrellas. This increase has nothing to do with cost; instead, it's all about the increased value that customers place on an immediately available haven from rain.

For many managers, the moral of this story represents a shift in the way they think about price. The insight of the fluctuating value of an umbrella is not just relevant to street vendors; it's applicable to every company in the world. No matter what product or service you sell, every pricing decision should be based on the value customers place on your product. You have to understand how customers value your product (as well as any optional features). Even minor services (e.g., custom or rush jobs) that may not cost you very much more to offer are like thunderstorm clouds on the horizon, signals that customers are willing to pay higher prices. How much hidden profit are you giving away because you are not increasing your prices at the first hint of rain?

Value: The Foundation of Pricing

One of the biggest fallacies in business is that a product's price should be based on its costs. Many companies set prices by simply adding a fixed markup on production costs. The problem with this approach is that it mistakenly assumes (intentionally or not) that customers base their willingness to pay for a product on how much it costs you to produce it. Costs had little to do with charging $3.95 for pet rocks[23] in the mid-'70s or the fact that baseball aficionados are willing to pay $100 for ticket stubs from the baseball game in which Cal Ripken broke Lou Gehrig's mark of playing 2,160 consecutive games.[24] Even though it costs the same, are you willing to pay the same price for a prime steak that you order medium-rare if it is served well-done? Customers choose the price they are willing to pay based on the value they *receive* from a product.

The good news is that simply changing the way you think about pricing can produce significant and immediate profit increases. The only role that costs should play is to act as a price floor. All value-based prices should at least cover a product's incremental costs. Other than that, it's all about value. Everyone needs to view pricing as a means to capture the value customers place on products. At a minimum, prices for those products that you "can't keep on the shelf" should go up on Monday morning.

When the global manufacturing company Emerson Electric implemented a value-based pricing strategy, it uncovered hidden profits. Jerry Bernstein, director of Emerson's price-improvement team, described his company's former pricing philosophy as follows: "You developed a product, looked at its costs, and said 'I need to make X.' You marked it up accordingly—and people would buy it."[25] In the late '90s, the company changed its pricing to focus on capturing the value customers placed on its products. This new perspective immediately uncovered hidden profits. For instance, an Emerson subsidiary (Fisher-Rosemount) that manufactured measurement devices benefited from value-based pricing. The company had developed a new sensor that measured fluid flows (to avoid pipes bursting or to ensure that mixtures had the correct proportions) at chemical manufacturing plants. Using its old cost-plus philosophy, these sensors would have been priced at $2,650. After highlighting and discussing the value of this new product (e.g., better accuracy and smaller size relative to competitors) with U.S. and European customers, Emerson's pricing team discovered that customers were willing to pay more than what they had planned to charge. In addition, they found that customers highly valued (and therefore were willing to pay a premium for) the Fisher-Rosemount brand name. Because of these factors, the final price was set at $3,150 and the company felt that profits were maximized. Had a lower price been charged, Fisher-Rosemount would have given away profits on each sale.

Shrimp is a product that benefits from a high perception of value. Because of the large influx of imports from shrimp farms in Asia and Latin America (now accounting for nearly 90% of the U.S. market), wholesale prices dropped by roughly 40% between 1997 and 2002.[26] Despite lower costs, retail shrimp prices remained relatively frozen. In fact, shrimp entrée prices at the Landry's Seafood House chain actually rose by 28% between 2000 and 2003. Although one explanation for this increase is that Landry's used bigger and better shrimp, CEO Tilman J. Fertitta conceded that his chain uses larger profits from shrimp to compensate for shrinking profits elsewhere.[27]

Despite shrimp surpassing canned tuna as the most popular seafood in the United States, these crustaceans are viewed by Americans as a luxury item that they expect to pay more for. This strong perception of value allows retailers to maintain or increase shrimp prices despite decreases in wholesale costs.

Thinking about price in terms of capturing value is the foundation of pricing for profits and growth. This insight alone can lead to greater profits on Monday morning, kudos from your boss, and a pat on the back from Wall Street in the form of higher share prices.

Caveats to Value-Based Pricing

For many, thinking about price in terms of value opens new opportunities to increase profits and grow. There are, however, a few caveats to keep in mind when setting value-based prices. For instance, there are occasions related to fairness and your company's overall strategy when value-based prices should be tempered. Competition also affects value. Sometimes I pause and enjoy a moment of fond satisfaction by thinking about all the great deals I capitalized on during the infancy of e-commerce competition. With companies like Buy.com viewing merchandise sales as loss leaders and promising the "lowest prices on earth," rivals had no choice but to offer similar deals.[28] Because of this intense competition, profits from the value these firms created were destroyed.

There are also, of course, situations in which fairness constrains a strategy of pricing. Raising prices after natural disasters (e.g., hurricanes and earthquakes) is a double-edged sword. At best, it represents an ethical dilemma about capturing the increased value customers place on products. At worst, well, you could be sent to jail. Chapter 9 discusses in greater detail the role that fairness plays in setting prices. It's an interesting dilemma. There is a point at which some products' values cross over to a position of power. They become "have-to-have" products. Even if a company gains this power, making a judgment on whether a price is fair depends on the product. Society probably shouldn't worry too much if a high price prevents teenagers from purchasing the latest "must-have" gadget. However, power over products associated with basic survival is more problematic. After a natural disaster, customers are willing to pay almost any price for basic supplies such as food, water, and shelter. In these types of cases, fairness is a compelling reason to restrain prices.

Gaining a reputation as a company that takes advantage of its customers during times of dire need can damage a brand. The 1994 Northridge, California, earthquake was the most expensive, in terms of financial damage, in U.S. history. After this quake, basic supplies like food and water were in high demand. A few 7-Eleven stores raised prices to capitalize on the increased value rattled residents placed on their products. After investigating several complaints of price gouging, 7-Eleven terminated eight Los Angeles–area franchises.[29] 7-Eleven did not want to be known as a company that takes advantage of its customers during natural disasters. In addition to losing their franchises, these store owners faced the possibility of criminal prosecution. After widespread reports of unfair pricing during the 1992 race riots, the city of Los Angeles enacted an ordinance prohibiting price gouging. For thirty days after a state of emergency is declared (earthquake, flood, fire, riot, storm, or natural or man-made disaster), it is illegal to raise prices by more than 10%. Each violation carries a maximum penalty of six months in jail and a $1,000 fine.

It's also important to not lose sight of your overall profit picture. Raising prices on *one* product can adversely affect *total* profits. Despite overwhelming demand, Sony never gave in to the temptation to raise prices on its PlayStation 2 video-game console. Supply shortages began with the PlayStation 2's roll-out in October 2000. Sony announced that due to production problems, it was only going to sell half of the million units it had promised to release in the United States. This announcement created a buying frenzy among customers eager to purchase this must-have holiday gift. Despite the opportunity to increase prices in this high demand/low supply environment, Sony maintained its suggested retail price of $299. As a result, enterprising middlemen began reselling their luckily acquired PlayStation 2 consoles on Internet auction sites like eBay. AuctionWatch.com (now operating as Vendio) reported that when the PlayStation 2 was released, its average selling price on auction sites was $950. By mid-December, after initial demand had been satisfied and supply had increased, the average auction selling price of $445 was still significantly above Sony's suggested retail price.[30]

Why didn't Sony raise prices in the face of this tremendous demand? The answer lies in the fact that the PlayStation 2 unit was only one component of Sony's profits. Sales of the PlayStation 2 base unit would lead to future revenues from individual game sales. When it was introduced, Sony had a brief window of opportunity in which it was the sole provider of advanced graphic video games. Competition from Microsoft's Xbox and Nintendo's GameCube game systems loomed on the horizon, and Sony wanted to capitalize on its good fortune by selling as many PlayStation 2 consoles as possible before these rivals crowded the market. If Sony had set a higher price, this price would become embedded in consumers' minds. How many times have you faced a high price and decided that the product is too expensive? Once customers make a judgment on a price, it's hard to change their minds. I am *still* trying to convince my father that cellular rates have dropped significantly. "The prices are crazy," he says incredulously whenever I bring up the idea of my parents getting a cell phone. He still remembers the $1-per-minute prices that prevailed when cellular service was introduced. Had Sony set higher prices and gradually lowered them, it would have taken a significant effort and—more important—time to convey the price reductions. Given the impending competition and the value of future game sales, Sony opted not to risk any sales delays. Maintaining the $299 suggested retail price allowed Sony to achieve maximum adoption of its PlayStation 2 platform. One additional benefit of this strategy was the resulting press coverage; media stories about shortages and frenzied purchasing behavior enhanced demand for the video-game system. A more complete discussion of the strategic reasons to amend value-based prices can be found in Chapter 9.

The final caveat regarding value-based pricing involves the role that competition plays in pricing. How are your rivals pricing? I recently discussed the virtues of value-based pricing with a friend of mine from college, George, who is now a lawyer. He immediately understood the concept and spoke excitedly about how his advice reduces his clients' tax bills. Why not price according to value, he reasoned, by charging 10% of the tax savings instead of billing for a few measly hours of time (at $200 an hour)? I felt a little bad about bursting George's rapidly growing bubble of riches by inquiring about how his competitors priced their services. As it turns out, many lawyers offer the same advice (and resulting tax savings), and they bill by the hour. Who would you want for your $20,000 tax savings—a lawyer who billed by the hour (two hours at $200 an hour) or one who charged 10% of what he saved you ($2,000)? If many sellers are offering similar products, your price is constrained by what your competitors charge.

Grow by Creating Value

Adopting the perspective of viewing products in terms of their value provides a platform for future growth. Your current products are loaded with growth potential. You should always be wondering, "What ancillary products will my customers value?" Or, even better, "What options will attract new customers?" These ancillary products are often less risky to create and can be even more profitable than your core product. Gaining insights into growth opportunities can be as easy as asking customers, "What do you like or dislike about my product?" Jaguar, for example, has created value for customers who buy the company's used cars. There's always uncertainty associated with purchasing a used car because of fears of hard-to-detect problems, the lack of warranty, and the chance that the car is a "lemon." Responding to these concerns, Jaguar created a Select Edition Certified Pre-Owned car program, available only at its dealerships. These used Jaguars pass a 140-point inspection, are restored to showroom-like quality, and come with an additional warranty. This popular program creates value (resulting in premium prices) by reducing the risks associated with buying a used car. Jaguar is an example of how growth can be generated by focusing on creating new value. The following are three common avenues to growth:

1. Enhanced Service

Offering enhanced services is another avenue to providing customer value. In this era of rising medical costs and incomprehensible medical pricing, the opportunity for doctors to grow their medical practice profits has been limited. A new trend, based on offering enhanced services, is changing this prognosis. Many doctors are opening boutique practices. A popular Midwestern physician recently changed his general practice to a membership-only service. Once serving close to twenty-seven hundred patients as part of a group practice, this doctor decided to open a solo practice limited to eight hundred patients. Now, the doctor is in only for patients who pay an annual out-of-pocket membership fee of $1,500. In addition to this fee, members are billed for office visits, tests, and other services. Private insurance and Medicare are accepted for these services. The benefits of membership include receiving same- or next-day appointments, no time limits on consultations, and 24/7 personal responses to health inquiries. While reducing the volume of patients will lower the doctor's income, membership fees alone could add up to $1.2 million a year in new revenue.[31]

The potential for profit also arises when customers want customized services. In July 2002, Jergens, the Cleveland-based industrial-equipment company, received an order from an aerospace parts maker for five hundred of its two-inch metal locking fasteners. These competitively produced two-inch fasteners are used to keep metal parts in position on industrial cutting and assembly machines. The aerospace company also requested ten customized one-and-three-quarter-inch versions of the fastener. Jergens company president Jack Schron said that in the past he would have absorbed the extra costs of making these specialized fasteners, selling all 510 at the same price as a loyalty gesture. This time, he calculated what it would cost to make the uniquely sized fasteners from scratch (setting up the machines to produce that size, overtime costs, etc.) and charged that amount. In actuality, he produced 510 full-size fasteners and shortened ten of them by a quarter of an inch. This was cheaper than interrupting production to recalibrate the factory machines.[32] This approach is a step in the right direction, and resulted in a healthy profit margin. That said, he probably could have charged even more had he focused on the value, not the costs, of the custom products.

2. Insurance

Many customers value insurance as a means to provide peace of mind. Extended warranties are a classic example of this type of insurance. For a fee that generally ranges between 10% to 30% of a product's price, an extended warranty promises a hassle-free fix of defects for a set term. These warranties are highly profitable add-ons to a company's core products. Britain's Consumer's Association, an independent organization dedicated to helping consumers make better-informed purchases, recently completed a study on extended warranties. The results were surprising. The Association found that extended warranties offered by the Dixons Group (Europe's leading electronics retailer) and Comet (a rival electronics company) accounted for 47% and 80%, respectively, of their pre-tax profits.[33]

Many consumer-interest groups criticize extended warranties as not worth buying. The healthy profits often generated from extended warranties are somehow translated into "ripping off" the consumer. The reality is that for any type of insurance provider, the sum of the repair costs has to be less than the total premiums received. Thus, the average consumer will pay more in premiums than they will receive in payouts. In line with the primary theme of this book, the decision to purchase an extended warranty should be based on how you value the product. Only you can decide how much you value peace of mind.

Quite frankly, I am not very technically savvy. We have all heard about people who build their own computers from scratch. I am exactly the opposite person. I get anxiety at the thought of merely adding new software to my computer. For this reason, I recently purchased extended/enhanced warranties on both my laptop computer and my printer. If there is a problem, I value the security of knowing that a technician will come to my house to fix it within twenty-four hours. For the record, the extended warranty on my laptop has paid off handsomely. For some reason, I take pleasure in knowing that more than $1,000 in repairs have been made to my laptop in the last few months. The extended-warranty provider for my printer is still winning (i.e., has not had to pay a repair claim) . . . but I still have a few more months to collect.

3. Financing

Offering financing provides an opportunity to compound your profits. Current customers are often your best bet for selling additional products to because they may well value the convenience of being able to purchase the full gamut of additional services and products from one company. In the case of General Motors, profits from ancillary products like financing dwarf those from its core operations. In the fourth quarter of 2003, profits from its finance operations (General Motors Acceptance Corporation) were $630 million. In that same quarter, worldwide profits from GM's vehicle operations were $396 million.[34]

In addition to adding profits, financing provides several marketing benefits. Most major retailers offer private-label credit cards that can only be used at their retail outlets. The relaxed credit standards associated with these cards can attract customers who are unable to qualify for a major revolving credit card. Furthermore, private-label credit cards allow customer purchases to be analyzed, which can provide insight into buying behavior and knowledge that can be used to create specialized promotions. In addition, since retailers control the credit cards, they can directly communicate (via advertising inserts) to their loyal customers. Finally, financing can be used to provide discounts without raising flags on a company's balance sheet. Promotions such as no payments for a year or 10% discounts for signing up for a credit card are implicit price cuts. On a company's balance sheet and communications to Wall Street, retail prices and sales appear robust, while the less-scrutinized credit-card division absorbs the financial consequences of these discounts.

Profit from Capturing Value

I'm contemplating creating an infomercial to support this book that will feature me screaming, nonstop, "Stop Giving the Value Away!" This mantra reflects a mindset that can unearth a wealth of hidden profits. A simple review of how customers value your products will create opportunities to increase profits.

The quickest path to uncovering hidden profits is to better understand and then charge for the value you provide. I get my hair cut at a funky barbershop down the street from my office, where rap music is blaring, incense is always burning, and usually a group of kids is gathered to discuss the latest MTV video. Then there is me . . . unfashionably clad in a sports jacket and (im)patiently waiting. I like the place, though. My barber is a real perfectionist, the location is convenient, and I admire his efforts to start a small business. The one drawback is the wait, which can be as long as ninety minutes. I was pleased when the shop started offering appointments in addition to serving walk-ins. My barber excitedly explained that he had finally built his customer base to the point where people would actually call to schedule appointments. The fact that customers were willing to schedule appointments was a real source of pride for him. Curious, I inquired whether this success and appointment option would change his pricing. A bit perplexed, he responded that the price was going to remain the same—regardless of whether the haircut was by appointment or walk-in. After our brief discussion on how customers value avoiding a long wait, the price of an appointment haircut instantly increased by $5. This was a perfect case of uncovering hidden profits—his costs did not increase, and the extra $5 was pure profit. While this was a pretty obvious move on the barber's part, my experience in working with companies is that opportunities for recovering untapped value are usually just as obvious. For example, when are electronic music companies (such as iTunes, which charges ninety-nine cents to download any song) going to start charging more for hit songs relative to songs that have little commercial appeal? Ask yourself: How much value are you giving away that your customers would willingly pay for?

It's helpful to remember that the power of price is rooted in its ability to change customer behavior. In planning my upcoming holiday travel, I discovered that I could save 33% on the airline ticket price by taking a seven-fifteen A.M. flight instead of my preferred nine-fifteen A.M. flight. Care to guess which flight I am *now* taking? The success that Hilton Hotels has enjoyed in using discounts to fill excess capacity further illustrates this power. Many of the chain's downtown hotels were thriving on weekdays (when businesspeople are in town) but abandoned on weekends. Who wants to spend the weekend in a city hotel? As it turns out, many customers are willing to do so if the price is right. Hilton started offering discounted BounceBack weekend rates, and within four years of implementing this program, Saturday went from being Hilton's second-lowest occupancy night to its highest.[35]

Never let a windfall pass you by. Sometimes, increases in the value that customers place on your product occur through no effort from you. The South Beach Diet is hot; with such luminaries as former president Bill Clinton crediting it with helping him to shed thirty-five pounds, the book promoting the diet has been a runaway *New York Times* bestseller. The diet is based on eating proteins and unprocessed carbohydrates and limiting the intake of processed carbohydrates. One of the diet's "approved" snacks is Laughing Cow cheese—a soft white cheese packaged in small wedges with a smiling red cow on the front of the package. This recommendation, made without the knowledge of the cheese maker, has created over-whelming demand for the product.

With retail prices ranging between $2.99 and $3.99, Laughing Cow is frequently sold out across the country. One Giant Food store in Annapolis, Maryland, has been com-pletely sold out for three months. A deli worker at the store described his customers as being "upset" at not being able to purchase the cheese. Information Resources Inc., a Chicago market-research firm, estimates that supermarket sales of the cheese increased by 56% in 2003. Laughing Cow claims that its light-cheese sales soared by 180% in March 2004 alone. On the auction site eBay, three packages of Laughing Cow Light (retail value $8.97–$11.97) are being sold for $23.99.[36] While benefiting from increased sales, choosing not to increase prices has resulted in the cheese maker—as well as its retailers—giving away a lot of hidden profits.

Businesses often opt to set the same prices at all of their locations. While this is easy to implement, it is important to understand the trade-off in profits that results from uniform pricing. Think about a jewelry-store chain with locations in Beverly Hills and Cincinnati. Should the prices of Seiko watches be the same at each location? If not, at which location should the prices be higher? Of course, you know I think the prices should differ. With respect to where prices should be higher, however, things aren't as clear-cut as you might think. For a moment, try to forget about the higher costs of operating in Beverly Hills. One reason prices could be higher in Beverly Hills is because movie stars and entertainment moguls can probably afford to pay more than watch fanatics in Cincinnati can. However, the competition between different watch brands in Beverly Hills is fierce. If there are fewer choices in Cincinnati, it is conceivable that customers will value a Seiko watch higher than their counterparts in Beverly Hills. The availability of substitute products is an important factor in determining price. Since the availability of substitutes is rarely the same in two areas, uniform pricing results in hidden profits.

Expanding Your Pricing Capabilities

Generous amounts of hidden profits can be uncovered by understanding that different customers have different valuations for the same product. I've already mentioned my fondness for Washington, D.C. To keep in tune with the latest hot spots there, I subscribe to *Washingtonian* magazine. The magazine has a subscription pricing structure that is designed to capture different customer valuations. A yearly subscription for readers living in the Washington area is $29.95. For U.S. subscribers not living in the D.C. metro area, the price is $39.95. Since postage and production costs do not differ for these customers, why the price differential? As with the case of the Beverly Hills vs. Cincinnati watch valuations, readers living outside of the Washington area have few alternatives for information about the city. In contrast, local residents have several information sources (e.g., local television, newspapers, etc.). Because of the lack of alternatives, out-of-town subscribers usually value the magazine more than local customers do. The *Washingtonian's* two-tier pricing strategy capitalizes on an easily definable segment's higher valuation of the magazine.

As a Boston resident, I am very interested in the pricing of Caribbean resorts, particularly in January. These resorts understand that in the winter, vacationers from snow-filled Boston tend to value a hotel room more than do travelers from sunny Florida who are seeking a weekend escape. To capture these different valuations, resorts often advertise different rates in different cities. Boston newspapers carry advertisements claiming a special $350 rate if you mention the promotional code "Boston" when calling the toll-free number. Similarly, Florida advertisements offer a $250 rate if you mention the promotional code "Florida." This advertising strategy allows resorts to capture different customer valuations for their rooms.

Understanding that different customers place different values on the same product or service is the most important concept in pricing. Once you accept this truism of value-based pricing, you expand the function that pricing performs for you—it's not finding a single perfect price number, it's about creating a series of strategies designed to capture the value each customer sets for your product or service. These strategies will uncover your product's hidden profits. In the next chapter, I will discuss in greater detail how customers set different values for products and services.

CHAPTER 4

Lessons from an Auction

Value Is in the Eye of the Beholder

It's natural to think, "Three-ninety-five for pet rocks? A hundred dollars for ticket stubs? Five thousand dollars for a lime-green couch? What's going on here? These prices are crazy!" This is the interesting facet of value: items that you and I may consider "junk," others will cheerfully pay for (I call this the "garage-sale syndrome"). The reason our valuations can widely vary from those of others is based on a variation on an ancient proverb: value is in the eye of the beholder. The value that we place on a product is a highly subjective judgment. Still not convinced? Let me share with you the story of an auction that took place in London not long ago.

In December 2002, Sotheby's hosted an auction to benefit Book Aid International. This charitable organization supports local initiatives to distribute books in forty of the world's poorest countries. Several prominent writers were asked to donate mementos that would be auctioned to support the charity's literacy drive.

The item that drew the most attention was a handwritten card from J. K. Rowling, the author of the popular *Harry Potter* book series. She donated a "teaser" index card that contained a string of ninety-three words that were clues to the plot of the highly anticipated fifth book in the series. Prospective bidders were not allowed to inspect the card or see the full text of the teaser. However, to tantalize the crowd, Sotheby's revealed that the following string of words was on the card: "thirty-eight chapters . . . might change . . . longest volume . . . Ron . . . broom . . . sacked . . . house-elf . . . new . . . teacher . . . dies . . . sorry."[37] Sotheby's set the pre-auction value of the teaser at £5,000 to £6,000.

At the time, the plot of the forthcoming *Harry Potter and the Order of the Phoenix* was a closely guarded secret. Rowling had remained uncharacteristically quiet about both the plot and the book's release date. This silence had stirred up rumors that she was suffering from writer's block. The secrecy surrounding the book, coupled with the popularity of the book series, created strong interest in the auction item and elicited some unusually devoted behavior from loyal fans. One Internet fan group, www.the-leaky-cauldron.org, even collected money from its members and promised to list the words on its website if it won the auction. This group collected £15,000 ($23,656) from more than fifteen hundred donors for its drive to purchase and publicize the secret ninety-three words.

The auction was frenetic. The bidding was so fast-paced that representatives of the Leaky Cauldron fan site did not even get to place a bid. The price shot past the club's healthy budget in less than a minute. An unnamed American collector won the auction with a bid of £28,680 ($45,231), close to five times higher than Sotheby's pre-auction estimate. Despite impassioned pleas from Harry Potter fans around the world, the winner never disclosed the ninety-three handwritten words.

For most of us, it's hard to believe that someone paid so much money for clues to a book that appeared eighteen months later. This auction reveals two key pricing concepts. First, value is truly in the eye of the beholder; second, and most important, the bidders' actions illustrate the most important concept in pricing . . . lessons from an auction.

Lessons from an Auction

Think about the bidding war that erupted for the Harry Potter teaser card or an auction that you have attended. The opening price is usually low enough to create a fast-paced one-upmanship between bidders. A lot of people are willing to participate when the price is low, hence the flurry of bids that pushed the Harry Potter teaser card price past $23,000 in less than a minute. But what I find so fascinating about auctions is the rationale that forces people to stop participating. As auctions heat up, participants slowly drop out. The price reaches a point where some bidders crumble and say, "This is too rich for my blood." Translated into pricing speak, this means, "It's not worth it to me anymore." The item is finally sold to the lone standing bidder, who announces with an air of triumph—sometimes tempered by a hint of buyer's remorse—that she is willing to pay more than anyone else in the room.

What's going on here? Everyone has the same information and is bidding on the same product. So why do some bidders drop out and others stay in? The answer is very straightforward: different people have different valuations for the same product. This commonsense notion is the lesson that any auction has to offer a pricing strategist. It's why some people, for example, willingly pay $278 for a serving of Tsar Imperial Beluga caviar while others would not consider eating—let alone paying for—this delicacy. Think about a sale item you recently purchased. Why did some people happily purchase the same item at the regular price, while you waited for a sale? They valued the product more than you do (lessons from an auction). Think about the stock market. Interestingly, at any price, both parties in a stock transaction—the buyer and the seller—think they are getting a good deal. The seller is happy to get out of the stock and put his capital into (hopefully) more fruitful investments. The buyer is pleased because of all the stocks that she evaluated, she thinks this stock is the most valuable for her portfolio. What's going on here? The stock market exists because of lessons from an auction. This important concept is clearly illustrated by watching bidders drop out of an auction at different price levels.

Understanding and capitalizing on the knowledge that for every product in the world, different customers will hold different valuations allows you to uncover your product's hidden profits. Everyone on board? Good . . . now let's go out and make some money.

The Superpower of Price

Before discussing how to expand your pricing capabilities with new strategies that are based on lessons from an auction, let's discuss how most of us currently use price. In our everyday business world, pricing behaves like an action hero. Just like Superman, pricing is powerful, swiftly achieves results, and can be summoned at a moment's notice. Having problems selling inventory? Cut the price. Customers lining up to buy your product? Hike up the price and use the profits to book that family trip to the Cayman Islands. Price is the final barrier to yes. All of us have faced that moment of uncertainty when a potential client says, "Your product is great; what's the price?" If you set the price too high, the thrilling aura of "I'm interested in buying" can instantly deteriorate into body language strongly suggesting "It's time for you to leave." (Believe me, I've been there and it's no fun.) A lower price, we reason, increases the chances of a deal and avoids this potentially embarrassing situation ("I'll see myself out"). "At least I'll make the sale," you say to yourself. "My numbers will go up, and I can justify the price break as 'goodwill' to my boss—hey, he falls for it all the time anyway." Price has the superpower to make or break a sale.

If you don't believe me, consider an experience I know we all share. A friend of mine swears that there is a "conspiracy" going on at Costco superstores. Like most people at these kinds of superstores, he always ends up leaving the store with far more merchandise than he had intended to buy. "Rafi, I can't get out of there for under two hundred dollars," he laments. So why do we always leave Costco with more merchandise than we thought we would buy? Price. The superstores' low prices (the chain pledges that its items will not be marked up by more than 14%) entices us to purchase products that we would not otherwise have considered. Just the other day, I was drawn to the opportunity to purchase thirty-two pounds of powdered laundry detergent for $9.99. It was just too good of a deal to pass up; I certainly didn't buy it for the convenience of carrying it up the stairs.

Price is so powerful because of its direct link to demand. Think of price as the hotline to market demand. High prices temper demand. Low prices stimulate demand. The siren song of a 50% discount can swiftly transform our "not interested" (at full price) into "I'll take it!" This well-known relationship between price and demand is the punchline of the previously discussed cornerstone of economics—the law of demand.

All businesses, to some extent, incorporate the law of demand into their pricing practices. For example, at retail stores prices start out high at the beginning of the season and eventually drop to make room for the next season's inventory. This is a timeless pricing strategy. Filene's Basement, a discount fashion retailer, openly uses the law of demand to move merchandise. All products are tagged with an initial price and a markdown schedule for the next thirty days. Merchandise is discounted after twelve selling days by 25%; after eighteen selling days the discount drops to 50%; and, finally, after twenty-four selling days, the price is trimmed by 75%. All items not sold after thirty days are donated to charity. Customers love this method of pricing. From the moment my father books a trip to visit me in Boston, I repeatedly hear the refrain, "We have to go to Filene's." Our bargain-hunting trips to Filene's usually conclude with him happily grinning in disbelief and saying something like "Look, this shirt still has the original tags from Barneys New York! It was selling for two hundred dollars at Barneys and I'm getting it for thirty dollars!" Never mind that he doesn't need a fancy shirt; he just loves the deal. For my dad, anyway, this is proof that money *can* buy happiness.

Of course, most managers are familiar with the law of demand. But this concept *alone* is not enough. The only way to price for profits and growth is to incorporate *both* the law of demand *and* lessons from an auction into your pricing strategy.

Pricing for Profits and Growth: Moving from Building Blocks to Tools

Once you've embraced the building blocks of pricing—price is based on value, lessons from an auction, and the law of demand—you have the foundation to price for profits and growth.

Traditionally, pricing has been viewed as the search for the perfect price. Even if this mythical price can somehow be found, everyone soon learns that there is room for improvement. You could just tell that some customers wouldn't have balked at purchasing if prices were higher, and more money could have been made from them. For other shoppers though, the indecision in their faces was obvious. They'd take a product off the shelf, stare at the price, and reluctantly return it to the shelf. A slight discount might have converted them into customers. Thus, the notion of "one perfect price" isn't optimal, it's difficult to implement, and it's riddled with missed profit opportunities. What will fill the gap is a multi-price mindset.

A multi-price mindset is a series of strategies that enables you to profit from each customer's unique product valuation. Remember those customers you thought would pay more? The multi-price mindset charges them higher prices, which they willingly pay. The multi-price mindset tips its hat to the law of demand by recognizing that lower prices will draw in new customers. Remember those shoppers who demurred because of price? The multi-price mindset discreetly offers them discounts. The multi-price mindset is the key to pricing for profits and growth for the following three reasons. First, price is aligned with value. If you aren't thinking about price in this manner, you are undoubtedly missing out on profits. Second, you'll make higher profits from the customers who value your product the most. Third, working in conjunction with the law of demand, the multi-price mindset increases your customer base through lower prices and offering new selling strategies. While you will earn fewer profits from these customers, you will nonetheless be earning additional, previously hidden profits.

The remainder of this book focuses on the three primary strategies that can be used to create a multi-price mindset: differential pricing, versioning, and segment-based pricing.

Differential pricing allows you to sell your product at different prices to different customers. For example, movie cinemas are adept at using differential pricing to attract customers with different valuations. To attract customers not willing to pay regular admission prices, discounts are offered to students, children, senior citizens, and customers with coupons. As a result, customers who often paid significantly different prices end up sitting next to one another, watching the same film.

Versioning offers a line of products, based on a core product, designed to attract new customers and implicitly reveal their valuations. For example, some products offer good, better, and best versions, with each level of quality priced differently. Versioning entices customers with lower valuations to purchase the lower-margined "good" product, and those with higher valuations to buy the premium-priced "best" product.

Most of us encounter this type of versioning once a week or so, when we decide whether to fill up with regular, plus, or premium gas.

Segment-based pricing strategies can target dormant customers and activate them. The idea behind this concept is that new pricing strategies will attract new customers. Sometimes the way you price is simply not appealing to interested customers (e.g., some may prefer to lease your product rather than buy it). For instance, the time-share pricing strategy has created tremendous growth in the vacation home–building industry by dividing vacation properties into fifty-two-week segments. Customers purchase a specific week, which is theirs for life. Time-share pricing targets customers who desire "owning" a vacation home but do not have the finances for or interest in making a full purchase.

The Multi-Price Mindset in Action

Few hotels fail to live the multi-price mindset—not that they can't do a better job of it, but they are usually well-versed in implementing multi-price mindset strategies. One of my favorite hotels is the Hyatt Regency Huntington Beach Resort and Spa. Cormac O'Modhrain, the general manager, is undoubtedly one of the nicest guys you'll ever meet. Cormac's hotel employs all three multi-price mindset strategies.

Differential Pricing. Customers calling Hyatt's toll-free reservations line are given a quote of $225 per night. Bargain hunters seeking a discounted rate can book online and save $10 with a nonrefundable "Internet only" price of $215. For travelers showing an AAA (American Automobile Association) card, the price drops to $202.50. Finally, seniors (aged sixty-two and over) can stay at the resort for $180. The hotel also offers a variety of discounted rates to guests on official government business and to corporations and conferences that pledge a minimum number of paid nights per year.

Versioning. The Hyatt offers several types of good, better, and best products at different prices. Regular rooms are categorized as "Guest," "Deluxe," and "Ocean View." Suite offerings range from Junior to Presidential.

Segment-Based Pricing. The hotel can be booked as part of a vacation package that includes airfare, accommodations, and car rental. The hotel also offers a $750 two-night "Romance Package" that includes accommodation in a suite, a bottle of champagne, a $100 food and beverage credit, and complimentary valet parking.

This multi-price mindset allows the Hyatt Regency Huntington Beach Resort and Spa to price for profits and growth. Its multi-price mindset attracts a wide spectrum of customers through targeted rates (i.e., seniors paying low rates relative to high rollers staying in the Presidential suite) and new pricing strategies (e.g., packages).

Compared to manufacturers, service-industry companies (e.g., restaurants and hotels) seem to be more proficient at incorporating elements of the multi-price mindset into their pricing. As I mentioned earlier, perhaps the daily pain of watching profits disappear (e.g., hotels with high vacancies) creates an extra incentive for service-industry companies to innovate their pricing. It's important to emphasize that the ideas in this book (specifically, lessons from an auction and the multi-price mindset) are relevant to every business in the world. Many manufacturers employ a multi-price mindset (several examples are highlighted in this book), but often do so less comprehensively than service companies do. Does this mean that the multi-price mindset is less applicable to product manufacturers? No, it just means that these businesses have more hidden profits to uncover. If your company manufactures products, you should be using the same pricing strategies you encounter at hotels, in restaurants, and on airlines.

Dell is an example of a product manufacturer that excels at pricing. This pricing expertise has helped Dell succeed in the highly competitive personal-computer market. One key to Dell's pricing success is that it has adopted a multi-price mindset by implementing the following strategies:

Differential Pricing. Dell divides its customers into four categories: home and home office; small business; medium and large company; and government, health care, and educational organizations. It tailors prices, promotions, and types of products offered to the category that each customer falls into. Additionally, Dell offers a variety of coupons (dis-

tributed via e-mail, regular mail, websites, and newspaper promotions) and rebates that price-sensitive customers can take advantage of.

Versioning. Dell has mastered the technique of versioning. While customizing their computers, customers are offered different choices of varying prices on a wide variety of components, including hard-drive capacity, processor speed, memory size, CD/DVD, and delivery options. The company also sells enhanced service plans such as next-day repair, spyware/virus removal, wireless home installation, and accidental-damage insurance.

Segment-Based Pricing. In addition to selling its products, Dell offers leasing plans. This targets customers who prefer leasing over making outright purchases. It also bundles products (e.g., a package containing computer, monitor, and printer) to attract customers who prefer the one-stop-shopping convenience of these bundles.

Much like the benefits that the Hyatt Regency Huntington Beach Resort and Spa reaps from using a multi-price mindset, Dell is able to serve a broad spectrum of customers and earn higher margins from some (ordering premium components and services) relative to others (buying bare-bones computers).

The remainder of this book focuses on expanding your pricing capabilities beyond that frustrating search for the perfect price point. Just like Hyatt and Dell, to price for profits and growth, you have to adopt a multi-price mindset.

What About Commodities?

The multi-price mindset also applies to commodities—undifferentiated products that most companies seemingly give up on in terms of innovative pricing. Mention the word *commodity* and most people almost reflexively start moaning about "low prices" and "no pricing power." Commodities are products that are identical in every aspect (characteristics, service, distribution, etc.) to those of your competitors. While there are few actual commodities in the market, many companies experience the unpleasant reality of their products becoming commoditized—they face market environments in which their products are losing pricing power. In this situation, companies selling commoditized products end up having their prices dictated to them by the rivals who are selling similar goods. If you don't match the competition, your customers will disappear. What's a manager to do?

If your product is becoming commoditized, I've got bad news for you. You have a strategy problem. Pricing cannot remedy this. You have to develop a new strategy (e.g., differentiation) that will distinguish your product and thus free your prices from their dependence on those of your competitors. Developing a new strategy is usually a significant and time-consuming endeavor. However, in the short term, creating a multi-price mindset can help you make the most of this unpleasant situation. While the long-term profit prospects will remain poor, at least you know you'll make more money tomorrow. Because customers have different valuations, even commoditized products can use the multi-price mindset to price for profits and growth.

"I love Netflix. It's the best!" is a surprisingly common refrain among my friends. Given their critical personalities, this is a hearty endorsement. Netflix came up with a truly great idea. As we all know, the two primary drawbacks of renting movies from a video store are the trips to pick up and drop off the videos, and those dreaded late fees. Netflix solved both problems. For a monthly fee, customers can keep three DVDs at a time for as long as they please (thus, no late fees). When they are finished with a DVD, they simply mail it back in the provided postage-prepaid envelope, and Netflix sends them (via U.S. Mail) the next movie on their Web-created request list. Travel to pick up and drop off videos is thus eliminated. The problem, however, is that Netflix's product is becoming commoditized. Companies like Blockbuster have started rival services, and Amazon.com is expected to enter the business in the near future.[38] As a result, Netflix has lost its pricing power, and its prices are literally being dictated by its rivals. Because of this competition, the company has recently been forced to drop its monthly price from $21.99 to $17.99.[39]

With little to differentiate itself from its powerful competitors, Netflix has a strategy problem. Its chances of ever regaining its pricing power are slim. If Netflix raises prices, many customers will defect. Likewise, if a competitor lowers its price, many Netflix customers will switch services. In this situation, sellers' prices are at the mercy of their rivals, and the intense competition usually drives down prices (and profits). But even in this unenviable business environment, lessons from an auction still apply. To price for profits and growth, Netflix can (and in many cases has started to) implement the following multi-price mindset strategies:

Differential Pricing. Coupons (via pop-up ads, mail, etc.) can be used to attract customers who have refrained from purchasing because the price has been too high for them. Customers who make the effort to redeem coupons are demonstrating that price is important to them.

Versioning. Netflix can use versioning to provide different types of services. In addition to its current policy of allowing customers to have three films at one time, it can also offer options to check out two (for a lower price) or four (for a higher price) movies. Also, instead of allowing a DVD to be held for an unlimited time (which is especially problematic when *everyone* wants the latest releases), Netflix can create a lower-priced option that limits the amount of time movies can be kept. Additionally, customers can pay a premium to receive priority preference (over regular customers) for their requested movies.

Segment-Based Pricing. In addition to offering its unlimited-usage subscription, Netflix can serve customers who value its convenience but do not want an unlimited supply of movies. For these customers, the company can offer two-week rentals (no long-term contract required). Higher-priced bundles (e.g., party packages that include popcorn and candy) can also be sold.

Even if all of Netflix's competitors copy its multi-price mindset pricing strategy, it is still better off. Consider the worst-case scenario. Suppose that all of Netflix's competitors adopt the same multi-price mindset pricing strategy. While the service will certainly not be as profitable as it would be if its rivals did not offer identical pricing, all companies will still earn higher profits. Each company will make more money because some customers will pay higher prices than others, and more customers will be served.

No matter what the product is, some people will get interested at a lower price and some will be willing to pay more. Lessons from an auction always apply. Therefore, the multi-price mindset is the key ingredient to pricing for profits and growth.

Fairness Revisited

After fully digesting the idea of the multi-price mindset, some people express hesitation about the fairness of charging different prices to different customers for the same (or a similar) product. Fairness in pricing was discussed earlier, but now is a good time to dig a little deeper into the issue. The multi-price mindset is about making more money from customers who value your product highly. But that's just one part of the multi-pricing strategy. You also have to find ways to discreetly offer lower prices to serve new, "price-conscious" customers. The result, of course, is that some customers pay more than others. Managers are often uneasy with this because they feel they are taking advantage of their best customers, and this uneasiness prevents them from using a multi-price mindset. As a result, they forgo hidden profits.

But consider this: the majority of multi-price mindset strategies are based on customer choice. Customers are offered a series of choices and prices. Do you want rush service or not? Do you want to fill your tank with regular, midgrade (Silver), or premium (Ultimate) BP gasoline? Is it worth it for you to search for, cut out, and carry coupons to a store to save twenty-five cents? Do you want to purchase a week in a time-share or buy a vacation home outright? Customers choose the product option that, given their valuations, provides them with the biggest bang for their dollar.

The role of fairness in differential pricing is more thought-provoking. When you call Southwest Airlines to ask for a fare quote, their reservations agents immediately ask, "Are all travelers between the ages of twenty-two and sixty-four? Is any traveler an active member of the military service?" Answers to these questions determine whether a traveler is eligible for one of Southwest's military, senior, youth, child, or infant discounts. Most of us are comfortable with these discounts because we feel that these customers deserve a discount. Other differential pricing avenues are less clear-cut. Should Web developers charge Fortune 500 companies higher prices for a snazzy website relative to what they charge small businesses just because the larger companies can afford it? What if small businesses reap higher benefits from showing their customers that they use the latest technology? Should small businesses be charged higher prices? Should a lawn service charge more to mow a lawn in an exclusive gated community than it does to mow a lawn of the same size for a customer who lives on the wrong side of the tracks?

Differential pricing is not unfair. Customers almost always have the right to say no to any price. A lawn service is welcome to quote whatever price it wants to homeowners residing in an exclusive area. However, they risk losing the contract to the enterprising kid next door who is willing to do the job for half the price with his family's riding lawn mower. Think back to the points raised in Chapter 2. When customers purchase from you, they are in essence saying, "Thank you; your product offers the best value relative to all of your competitors." Is this thank-you accompanied by an implicit contract that limits your profits? Only you can make this judgment.

CHAPTER 5

The Value Decoder

The Fickle Nature of Value

To own or not own a car is a decision that people living in cities like Boston or New York usually face at some point in their lives. Suppose you face this dilemma. Since it's generally easy to get around in a city (using public transportation, taking taxis, or walking), for the most part owning a car is not a necessity (certainly less so relative to those living in distant suburbs). This purchase decision is truly based on your understanding of how much you value owning a car. How much do you value the convenience of having a car to go to the grocery store and to run local errands? How much does it mean to you to be able to drive to visit your friends, who are increasingly moving to the suburbs? Finally, how much do you value owning the latest luxury sedan or can you be content, as I used to be, with driving around town in a rusty, $300, 1972 Volvo?

Suppose a well-off friend of yours is leaving the country and needs to sell her new BMW 325xi (market value: $32,000). Not wanting to deal with the hassle of placing an ad in the newspaper or negotiating with used-car dealers, she generously offers to sell you the car for "whatever you think it's worth." How much will you offer—$10,000, $20,000, $32,000?

- What if a rental-car agency opens up down the block and rents cars for $60 on weekdays and $35 on weekends? Would that change how much you are willing to pay? *The price and availability of substitutes affect value.*

- Suppose a coworker is selling a 1985 Honda Civic—basic transportation—for $1,500. Will this potential substitute influence the amount you are willing to pay for your friend's BMW? *The characteristics of a product relative to its competitors' affect value.*

- What if you learn that you just got that long-awaited promotion, which is accompanied by a 25% raise? Will this affect the amount you are willing to pay? *Income affects how you value a product.*

- Suppose auto-insurance companies announce that annual premiums will rise by 15% next year. Will this sway the price you are willing to pay? *The availability and price of related products affect value.*

- What if the city council passes an ordinance requiring alternate-day parking? This regulation requires cars to be parked on only one side of the street, and the authorized side changes every day. As a result, every day you'll experience the joy of finding a new parking spot on the opposite side of the street. *Changes in market environment affect value.*

This city dwellers' auto-purchase dilemma illustrates two important points about value. First, there are several components that make up and influence value. Second, a change in any of these components affects value. The value you place on a slightly used BMW 325xi will change if the nearby rental-car agency lowers its prices by 50%; or your coworker ups the price of his 1985 Honda Civic to $3,000; or your promotion is only accompanied by a 10% raise; or you get a speeding ticket that results in a 20% jump in your insurance premium; or a new supermarket opens in your neighborhood.

In my line of work, helping companies with their pricing strategy, I hear people use the word *value* all the time. *Value* is an easy word to understand because we calculate it daily in our lives. For every purchase we consider, we judge value: the Vtech cordless phone *is* worth $79.99; the Belgian Flip Waffle Maker is *not* worth $129.99. Sure, we all get the concept. But when I ask people at dinner parties how they calculate value, they become uncomfortable. "I don't know, I just do it," they respond with a hint of annoyance as they anxiously seek refuge in a nearby conversation. My point is that while it is essential for companies to understand how customers value their products, few actually do. Because calculating value is almost reflexive to us, many people in business automatically think, "I understand value," and just take the concept for granted. This lackadaisical attitude results in hidden profits; companies do not really understand how customers value their products or what factors change these valuations.

In this chapter, I am going to dissect for you what's going on in our minds when we make a snap decision about a product's value. Understanding how customers calculate value uncovers your hidden profits in three key ways. First, remember the central idea of Chapter 3: it's all about value. The tools in this chapter will help you set prices that best reflect the values that customers place on your product. Second, if you better understand how customers determine value, you'll gain insight into how to increase your product's value. Finally, as was shown in the example of the car-buying decision, a product's value can instantly change due to circumstances beyond your control (e.g., other car-purchasing options materialize, insurance premiums change, new parking regulations are introduced). Pricing for profits and growth means constantly aligning prices with any shifts in your product's value. I'm going to show you what price-changing forces to be on the lookout for.

The Value Decoder

The Value Decoder is a framework for determining a product's value. It enables you to analyze the components that make up value, and then shows you how to translate this analysis into the right price for your product.

Figure 5-1 The Value Decoder

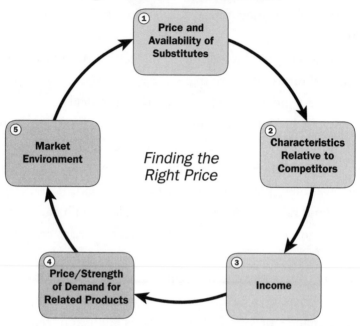

The Value Decoder, however, is not a formula into which you can plug a few inputs and out pops your product's perfect price. Since you ultimately have to set a numerical price ($18 or $31), the desire to focus on getting the numbers exactly right is understandable. Just like most of us have come to terms with the fact that we will not return to the same size of blue jeans that we wore in high school, you have to accept that there is no surefire way to find your product's optimal price. But with the right research and judgments, the Value Decoder minimizes the error in setting price—it provides the best opportunity to come close to finding the right price for your product and each of its multi-price mindset strategies. In the end, will your prices be off by a percent or two? Probably.

The Value Decoder breaks down value into the five components (listed in Figure 5-1) highlighted in the earlier discussion of city dwellers valuing a car. The first two ("Price and Availability of Substitutes" and "Characteristics Relative to Competitors") are the most important in determining customer value. For example, when you are buying a stereo, what do you really look for? As any good consumer should do, for my recent stereo purchase I visited several stores (e.g., Best Buy, Circuit City, Bang & Olufsen) to see which stereos fit my budget, noted the unique characteristics of the models that interested me, and then compared prices. In the end, I selected the stereo that offered the combination of attributes and price that were best for me. So while I paid more for a CD player that stores four hundred CDs, I decided that the premium associated with the stylishly designed Bang & Olufsen stereos were not worth it to me. The remaining three components of value (Income, Price/Strength of Demand for Related Products, and Market Environment) are important, but they really come into play in understanding how a product's value can change. For example, an inheritance from a distant relative may raise the amount I'm willing to pay for a stereo (income affects value); a 25% jump in CD prices may lower how I value a four-hundred-CD-capacity player (price of related products affect value); or the widespread adoption of electronic music such as MP3s may make me value a CD player less (market environment affects value).

Value Decoder Analysis for a Single-Engine Aircraft

Suppose that you are the CEO of New Design, a startup manufacturer of single-engine aircraft. You are entering the market with an airplane that has the potential to be a bestseller because of its advanced aerodynamic design (which allows better fuel efficiency and faster cruising speeds), wider cabin, and enhanced safety features. The problem is that you've been waking up in the middle of the night wondering what price you should charge for your new product. The following five-step process shows how a Value Decoder analysis can determine the right price for New Design's airplane (as well as help you sleep better).

Step 1 (Price and Availability of Substitutes). The first step in any Value Decoder analysis is to identify potential substitutes for your product. These substitutes are what customers will compare your product to. In New Design's case, the product competes against aircraft produced by an industry stalwart, Popular Plane. Popular Plane manufactures a rival single-engine plane that is priced at $340,000.

Step 2 (Characteristics Relative to Competitors). The next step is to understand how your product measures up, in terms of attributes, against those of your rivals. Performance is what really distinguishes New Design's

airplane. Compared to Popular Plane's aircraft, New Design's plane has a faster cruising speed (185 knots vs. 158), a longer cruising range (1,100 nautical miles vs. 886), and a faster climb rate (1,400 feet per minute vs. 1,040). New Design's plane also has a revolutionary safety system not offered by any competitor: in the event of an extreme in-flight emergency, a parachute can be deployed that will safely lower the airplane to the ground (while you may think this device is a product of my vivid imagination, this safety feature is actually standard on all airplanes manufactured by Cirrus Design). However, customers tend to value Popular Plane's brand higher than they do New Design's. Popular Plane was started nearly eighty years ago. Understandably, buyers value its strong heritage, its reputation as an industry leader, and its reliability.

Companies have to understand how customers value their product's differences (relative to competitors) and price accordingly. Suppose your pricing team finds that because of the enhanced performance of New Design's plane, it can charge a $70,000 premium, as well as an additional $35,000 for its revolutionary safety features. However, it needs to discount its price by $15,000 since its brand is not as highly valued as Popular Plane's.

Step 3 (Income). Income plays an important role in a product's value. As income increases, consumers are generally willing to pay more for a product. To help support his constituency, a senator from Wyoming, where New Design has its headquarters and manufacturing plant, pushed a $25,000 single-engine-airplane tax credit through Congress for owners of aircraft with enhanced safety equipment. Of course, since only New Design's aircraft have these safety features, their customers alone benefit from this congressional largesse. Because of this tax credit, customers are willing to pay an additional $25,000 for a New Design plane.

Step 4 (Price/Strength of Demand for Related Products). The prices of related products are important in determining value. For example, suppose a recent increase in airport landing fees affects the value customers place on owning planes, as airplanes become more expensive to operate. To compensate for these higher operating costs, your pricing team finds that prices of all private planes should be lowered by $20,000 to maintain customer demand.

Step 5 (Market Environment). There are other variables, which I term *market environment,* that affect value. For instance, consider how a public-relations campaign by a private-aircraft industry group (coalition of manufacturers) can benefit value. Suppose this publicity campaign highlights the convenience (no more lines at the airport), ease, and thrill of flying a private plane. The resulting enhanced stature of owning a plane (it's the "in thing" to do) allows manufacturers to increase prices by $10,000.

Figure 5-2
New Design's Value Decoder Analysis

STEP 1	Price and Availability of Substitutes	$340,000
	• *Popular Plane's price*	
STEP 2	Characteristics Relative to Competitors	
	• *Add $75K for performance attributes and $30K for safety features*	$105,000
	• *Subtract $15K because of less-desirable brand name*	($15,000)
STEP 3	Income	
	• *Add $25K due to tax breaks*	$25,000
STEP 4	Price/Strength of Demand for Related Products	
	• *Subtract $20K because of higher landing fees*	($20,000)
STEP 5	Market Environment	
	• *Add $10K because of public-relations campaign*	$10,000
	New Design Aircraft Price	**$445,000**

The Conclusion

New Design's High-Performance Aircraft Pricing Analysis. Given that consumers always have the choice to buy a single-engine aircraft from Popular Plane, its $340,000 price is the base from which New Design should build its price. The following premiums can be added to this base price: $70,000 (enhanced performance),

$35,000 (safety features), $25,000 (tax credit), and $10,000 (public-relations campaign). However, the following deductions must be made: $15,000 (less-desirable brand name) and $20,000 (to compensate for higher landing fees). Starting with the $340,000 base price and adjusting it to account for these factors leads to a $445,000 price tag for New Design's airplane.

As you can see, the Value Decoder framework makes determining price a well-reasoned and transparent process. Every factor that affects value is clearly identified and incorporated into price. The remainder of this chapter guides you through the five-step Value Decoder process, discusses each component of value in detail, and shows you how to put the five components of value together to find your right price.

Step 1:
Price and Availability of Substitutes

Your price is based on what close competitors are charging. How much are they charging? If they change their prices, how will you change yours? How will competitors react if you change your price?

The number-one theorem in pricing is that your competitor's price affects how consumers value your product. Robert Crandall, American Airlines' former chairman and CEO, best summed up the central role that competitors have on setting prices: "This industry [airline] is always at the grip of its dumbest competitors."[40] The fact is that you may have a great product, but if competitors set ridiculously low prices, customers are going to value your product less (a lesson that many e-commerce companies learned during the early stages of the Internet).

The intense rivalry between Jay Gould's Erie Railroad and Commodore Cornelius Vanderbilt's Central Railroad in the nineteenth century illustrates the pivotal role that competition plays in determining value. These adversaries battled to control livestock transportation between Buffalo and New York City in 1867. The standard price for the route was $125 per carload. Vanderbilt incited a price war by reducing his rate to $100; Gould responded with another $25 price cut. The Commodore reciprocated; Gould struck back by dropping his price to $25. When Vanderbilt set his price at $1 per carload, Jay Gould's Erie cars ran empty, and Vanderbilt celebrated his victory—given that both railroads offered virtually the same service, why would customers pay more to Gould?

The Commodore's merriment abruptly ended, however, when he discovered that Gould had purchased every steer in Buffalo and sent them for slaughter in New York on Vanderbilt's rail cars—yielding large profits for Gould, quite literally at the Commodore's expense. Moreover, in the process, Vanderbilt's aggressiveness wiped out a profitable business.[41] This story illustrates how little control you have over your own product's value. Despite your best intentions, your competitors' prices will heavily influence your pricing.

Step 2: Characteristics Relative to Competitors

List all of your product's competitors. How does your product stack up to these rivals in terms of the six characteristics discussed in this section: brand, convenience, quality, attributes, service, and style? Accounting for these differences in characteristics, what price premium (or discount) should you set relative to these competitors?

Customers will always compare your product's value with the competition's as long as they are viable purchasing options. Remember George, my lawyer friend from Chapter 3 who wanted to charge a fee equal to 10% of his clients' tax savings? The foil to his dream of riches was the fact that many of his competitors (rival lawyers) charge lower prices. If George offers an indistinguishable service, his price is constrained by what his rivals are charging. However, my friend's value changes if he has unique characteristics relative to his competitors. Perhaps he is more experienced or works for a prestigious law firm. In this case, customers will value George's services by reasoning, "I can use any tax lawyer for two hundred dollars an hour. How much more do I value solid experience or a powerful law firm's brand name?" (I, of course, have switched tax lawyers and am paying only $150 an hour. George is not that good a friend.)

For most products, it's easy to find competing products to use as the basis for determining value. After identifying competing products, you have to understand what distinguishes your product. It's these differences that affect how customers value your product. Six categories of characteristics that distinguish your product from others are:

1. Brand

Brands can differentiate a product. A brand is a perception in the minds of customers that generally conveys trust, quality, and/or style. The Shanghai Tobacco Corp., a Chinese cigarette manufacturer, has profited from the fact that brands influence value. Customers line up for as long as twelve hours to pay $10—a price that is as much as sixty times more than competitors charge—for a pack of Panda cigarettes. These cigarettes are highly coveted symbols of luxury. The brand's popularity is rooted in the late Chinese leader Deng Xiaoping's love for Panda cigarettes. Throughout his career, he was usually photographed with a Panda in hand. Although the cigarettes were previously limited to the political and military elite, after Deng's death in 1997 the manufacturer began selling limited quantities to the public. Curiously, most buyers do not actually smoke the cigarettes. Instead, they use them as symbols of fine taste to curry favor among friends, superiors, or officials. Many recipients proudly display the classy cigarettes on their desks as a sign of prestige. Shanghai Tobacco admits that its customers often purchase Pandas to satiate their "VIP complex."[42]

2. Convenience

Convenience can affect value. A common complaint heard from rock-concert fans concerns the ubiquitous "convenience charge" that is added to tickets purchased through the Ticketmaster service. This surcharge typically ranges between 5% and 10% of the ticket's price. But really, what could be easier than picking up the phone (or logging on to Ticketmaster's website), ordering your tickets, and having them mailed to you? To avoid Ticketmaster's service fees, fans usually have the option to drive to the venue on the day that tickets go on sale, stand in line, and purchase tickets directly from the box office, but few do so. Complaints notwithstanding, Ticketmaster provides a convenience that customers willingly pay for.

3. Quality

Every day we face choices about quality; it's an important characteristic customers use to evaluate products. I can still vividly remember pleading with my mother in 1979 to buy me a pair of the winter hiking boots all my friends were wearing. The $50 price tag at Sears held her back. I finally persuaded her by highlighting the boots' long-lasting quality and agreeing to buy a larger size. I still have those boots, and they still look great. Every year, after putting on the boots during the first snow, I call my mom to remind her of what a high-quality purchase we made.

Higher quality does not imply a lock on customers, though. Customers often are not willing to pay the higher price that is usually associated with improved quality. I use a dry-cleaning service that offers daily pickup and delivery at low prices. While the owner is a nice guy, let's just say that customer service is not his forte. Without fail, twice a year I have to call to complain about white splotches (from the dry-cleaning process) that are all over my shirts. The negotiation typically begins with him angrily screaming, "It's your fault," and concludes with him redoing the shirts to my satisfaction. Sometimes, when I am not in the mood for conflict, I think about using a more reputable company. But these other services charge close to double what I currently pay. Even though I have higher-quality options, I've decided that despite his attitude and the occasional white splotch, my dry cleaner offers me the best value.

4. Attributes

Have you shopped for a cell phone recently? What a myriad of choices! Cell phones come with features like cameras, electronic games, schedulers, Internet access, text messengers, music players, and television screens. These features can be so overwhelming that it is easy to lose sight of the device's primary purpose—making phone calls. What's going on here? Cell-phone manufacturers understand that attributes can distinguish their products, and this affects how customers value their phones.

5. Service

For many, service strongly influences value. The long-defunct carrier Eastern Airlines uniquely used service to enhance the value of its Northeast corridor (Boston–New York–Washington, D.C.) shuttle service. The close proximity of the three cities, high traffic volume, and business travelers' constantly changing schedules provided the company with an opportunity to innovatively create value. The airline distinguished itself by guaranteeing passengers a seat on any of its scheduled shuttles. If one shuttle filled up, Eastern pledged to roll out a new plane—even if it was for only one passenger. Passengers loved this service. Last-minute flight? Meeting done early? Want to take the Friday, five P.M. shuttle? No problem. Adding new planes to accommodate additional passengers was not just a clever marketing idea; it was a profitable daily occurrence. On some days, as many as seventy-two additional planes were rolled out to satisfy the overwhelming demand.[43]

And yes, a new plane was rolled out solely to fly one passenger about fifty times in the shuttle's history.[44] The first occurrence of a single-traveler flight drew spectacular publicity. The image of a lonely passenger in a spacious plane indelibly conveyed Eastern's high level of service. This guarantee helped Eastern to profitably dominate East Coast air travel for over a quarter of a century.

6. Style

Lloyd Hansen, the Vice President of Revenue Management at Ford, understands that style affects value. When he sells Ford's inventory of returned leased vehicles (more than a million cars annually), he charges different prices based on the color of the car. In hot climates like Arizona, dark-colored cars are less popular because they attract heat. In these areas, Lloyd sets higher prices for white cars. Conversely, higher prices are charged for the luxurious look of black prized in cities like New York.[45]

Now that you know how your product rates (in terms of characteristics) relative to your competitors', it's easy to see the pivotal role that rivals' prices play in value. If your product offers the fewest attributes, its price must be lower than those of your rivals. Even if your product is considered high-end, you have to watch your competitors' prices. If the price differential becomes too large, some customers will begin reasoning, "The premium attributes aren't worth the price differential; I am going downscale." Think about a brand-name product you buy (e.g., Levi's jeans). What's your tipping point, in terms of the largest price differential that you'll accept, before you shun your beloved Levi's for a pair of private-label jeans?

There are some unique products where, admittedly, it's difficult to use competing products as a basis for value. For example, Sir Richard Branson recently announced the formation of Virgin Galactic, a company that is offering customers the unique opportunity to travel into space. For $207,000, well-heeled travelers can board a rocket ship for a suborbital flight (just outside the Earth's atmosphere).[46] What competing products can be used to value the experience and stories that can be told of flying approximately sixty-two miles above Earth? Perhaps you can use the $20 million figure that private citizens have paid to travel on Russian Soyuz space capsules.[47] Alternatively, the right comparison may be a luxurious vacation. The luxury-tour operator Abercombie & Kent offers, for $39,985, "A Connoisseurs Europe" trip that includes travel in a private, reconfigured 757 jet, among other premium amenities.

One way to more accurately value these unique products is to shift the onus to consumers by using an auction. In 2003, the privilege to lunch with legendary billionaire investor Warren Buffett was auctioned off to benefit charity. The winner, Greenlight Capital founder David Einhorn, paid $250,100 for the privilege of meeting the legendary capitalist, whose investment style mirrors the word emblazoned on his personalized license plate—THRIFTY. Commenting on the experience through a spokesperson, Mr. Einhorn praised the meal as "a once-in-a-lifetime opportunity to meet Mr. Buffett and contribute to a great cause."[48]

Step 3:
Income

How much money do your customers make? How does their income affect the price they are willing to pay for your product?

As a general rule, the higher a person's income, the more he will value a product. Warren Buffett probably values his daily *Wall Street Journal* more than most other readers do. Think about a product that you have refrained from purchasing because of its high price. Would you be as hawkish on price if you received an unexpected six-figure inheritance from a distant relative? If your customers are rich, there's probably some wiggle room to increase your margins. But if your customers are watching every penny, they will be sensitive to the slightest increase in price.

Sellers have to recognize that changes in their customers' incomes affect value. A tax cut to the middle class may make these customers willing to pay more to rent a vacation condominium in Florida. Conversely, if your customers are rich investment bankers, a bad year on Wall Street may make them negotiate harder for their summer-house rentals in the Hamptons.

Step 4:
Price/Strength of Demand for Related Products

What other goods affect your product's value? What effect do these products have on your product's value (e.g., if their price goes down, how does the value of your product change)?

When two goods are bought in tandem, like gasoline and cars, the price of one product often affects how consumers value the other. For instance, as gasoline prices creep above $2 per gallon in the United States, gas guzzlers are becoming less appealing. High gas prices make it more expensive to operate large vehicles like SUVs. Owners of Hummer SUVs, for example, are beginning to feel the pinch. One driver, a New York hedge-fund owner, complained that he spends $60 to fill up his Hummer and is thinking about trading it in.[49] Even the rap star Coolio is keeping an eye on his Hummer's gas mileage: "I've got two [gas] tanks and it takes three to get to San Francisco. Over the years, that adds up," he recently fretted.[50] Rumored to have only high-single-digit gas mileage (since Hummers weigh so much—over three tons—they are exempt from mileage-reporting requirements), demand is waning. Sales in 2004 of the H1 and H2 model Hummers were down 65% and 27%, respectively, compared to 2003 figures.[51]

Step 5:
Market Environment

What changes in the market environment (fad, new information, unexpected event, timing) affects your product's value? Which of these market-environment changes are predictable? What others have a high probability of occurring?

Finally, market-environment variables (market occurrences that are out of your control) contribute to your product's value, both positively and negatively. Sometimes, a company can wake up to find its product's value drastically changed because of a fad, new information, an unexpected event, or simple timing. For example, on November 17, 1991, the CBS television show *60 Minutes* ran a story titled "The French Paradox." The story focused on the fact that despite having a diet high in fat and cholesterol, the incidence of heart disease among the French is significantly lower than for Americans. One doctor interviewed on the program claimed that a moderate intake of alcohol reduces chances of coronary disease by as much as 50%. After the show was broadcast, the French government took out full-page advertisements in newspapers summarizing the *60 Minutes* piece with the declaration that "the intake of fat in the French diet seems to be counteracted by drinking French wine."[52] This increased the value of wine. Four weeks after the *60 Minutes* report was aired, sales of red wine surged by 44% in U.S. supermarkets.[53] In addition to new information (e.g., The French Paradox), other examples of market-environment changes include the Atkins Diet lowering the value of high-carbohydrate foods like pasta while increasing the value of meat products (fads); the local baseball team winning the pennant, so now the World Series is coming to town (unexpected event); and Christmas trees being more valuable on December 24 than on December 26 (timing).

Putting It All Together

The final step in the Value Decoder framework involves evaluating each of the five components and then setting your price. Just as we worked through the Value Decoder analysis for New Design's single-engine plane, I suggest that you create a presentation that has six sections—one for each of the five Value Decoder steps, and a sixth section for your final conclusion. In each of the five component sections, list all relevant analysis, data, market research, and expert opinions. At the end of each section, summarize your reasoning based on its relevance to your product's value. In the sixth section (the conclusion), you should construct your argument, based on the five Value Decoder steps, to justify your price recommendation.

Let me go one step further and suggest that you present your Value Decoder analysis to everyone in your company.

Pricing is just that important. The pressure of a company-wide presentation will push your pricing team to do its best work in terms of precision, clear logic, and amassing persuasive backup data to find the price that best reflects your product's value. Just as important, this presentation signals to your employees that price matters and allows them to confidently convey your product's worth to customers.

While the Value Decoder framework requires much more effort than the murky reasoning often used at hastily called "pricing meetings," the analysis offers you the best opportunity to get your price right and realize hidden profits. The transparent and structured process of the Value Decoder methodologically searches for every possible source of value in your product. This also allows everyone to better understand the product's value. A clearly articulated, data-backed value analysis is the key to pricing for profits and growth.

Finally, the Value Decoder highlights what few realize: you have little control over your product's value. With the exception of two variables—your product's characteristics and prices—most of the factors that establish value are determined by other forces. Your product's value is at the mercy of these constantly fluctuating factors. If your price does not incorporate the factors that you don't control, it will not accurately reflect your product's value. By highlighting what external variables (e.g., income, related products, etc.) you should be monitoring, the Value Decoder allows you to keep your price aligned with your product's value.

Explaining Lessons from an Auction

Recall this book's central idea: hidden profits can be realized by understanding and capitalizing on the fact that different customers place different values on a product. After presenting the Value Decoder framework, I can better illustrate why customers have different valuations for the same product. As you can see, every single element of the Value Decoder involves subjective consumer decisions. Is the Fila brand worth 25% more than the Nike swoosh? Does the usual 30% price hike around Valentine's Day stop you from purchasing a dozen red roses? Will a buy-one-get-one-free sale on hamburger buns compel you to purchase more hamburger? Will that long-hoped-for 10% raise allow you to go on a dream vacation? How low do private-label soda prices have to drop for you to stop buying Pepsi?

Every facet of *every* component of value is driven by *every* consumer's subjective judgment. Think about how diverse people are. It would be surprising to find two people who value the same product identically. Still don't believe me? Pick any item in the latest Sharper Image catalog and ask your friends what price they would be willing to pay for it. My bet is that no one's price will match. To go one step further, I'd bet that their prices won't even be close to one another's. The highly subjective nature of value is the reason product valuations vary so widely.

CHAPTER 6

Differential Pricing

X-ray Vision

When I was a kid, I was intrigued by a comic-book advertisement for Slimline's X-ray Specs. The headline trumpeted AMAZING ILLUSORY X-RAY VISION INSTANTLY. For those who did not read the fine print closely, like me, the advertisement implied that the glasses would let you experience x-ray vision. "What fun," I thought! So I saved my allowance and sent $1, plus twenty-five cents for shipping (even Slimline understood versioning; I could have purchased the deluxe model for $2), to the P.O. Box listed in the ad. Two weeks later, I received a package in the mail. Shortly after putting on the "X-ray Specs," I came to understand what the word *illusory* meant. That said, Slimline did live up to its promise: the glasses lasted for years, needed no batteries, and were completely harmless. I recently found a gag shop that sells the same glasses (the price has since increased to $3.99), and their description puts it best: "The real gag of these specs is that the rest of the world has the sneaking suspicion that they actually might work."[54]

Every day you interact with shoppers who are willing to pay you more money or who could be converted to customers if only the price were lower. Wouldn't it be great if you had x-ray vision that allowed you to see how much each customer was willing to pay so you could discreetly offer them a price that matched their valuation? I am going to show you exactly how to do this. The techniques in this chapter will enable you to differential price—the ability to uncover and act upon the different values customers place on your products and services. This component of a multi-price mindset strategy enables you to sell the *same* products to *different* customers at *different* prices. And I promise you, there is nothing illusory about the profits this strategy will generate.

There are seven differential-pricing techniques:

1. Customer Characteristics. Age, gender, organization affiliations, and proximity to an attraction are characteristics that can be used to identify customers with different valuations, and allow you to offer them different prices.

2. Hurdles. Coupons, sales, memberships, size, and conscious actions are hurdles that can help you identify and sell products to customers with different valuations.

3. Time. Incorporating the notion of time into pricing can allow you to capitalize on customers willing to pay a pre-

mium to have a product immediately, as well as those with lower valuations who are willing to wait for lower prices.

4. Quantity. Lower prices can be used as an incentive for customers to purchase larger quantities of a product.

5. Distribution. Different prices can be charged based on where customers make purchases.

6. Mixed Bundling. Selling products both individually and in discounted bundles can enable you to charge different prices to different customers.

7. Negotiation. Individually negotiating with customers can lead to your charging different product prices.

Customer Characteristics

Customer characteristics provide clues about the valuations individuals place on a product and, therefore, the level of price they may be willing to pay. As you think about your customers, what characteristics distinguish their valuations? Can age, the reason amusement parks offer discounts to seniors and children, be used to identify those with lower valuations? How about the type of company? The organization (e.g., nonprofit, government, educational, small vs. large businesses, etc.) making the purchase often reveals a lot about their willingness and ability to pay.

Gender is a controversial characteristic used to identify customer valuation. For example, dry cleaners notoriously charge higher prices to clean a woman's shirt, despite the fact that it is virtually no different from a man's. The price for a "men's shirt" is $1.65. However, if a similar shirt is tagged "women's blouse," the price jumps to $5.25.[55] Is the value that women place on a wrinkle-free shirt really that much more than what men are willing to pay? Apparently so. Victoria's Secret has also experimented with gendered pricing. In 1996, customers discovered that men were being offered lower prices than women. Prices were differentiated by a promotion listed in the company's winter catalog. One female recipient's catalog included a "$10 off a purchase of $75 or more" coupon. On the same day she received her catalog, a male received a catalog that listed the same prices but had a different promotion: his catalog offered a $25 discount on a purchase of $75 or more.[56] Gender pricing capitalizes on the obvious: women value women's clothes more than men do. However, one could argue the contrary. Men may be less price-sensitive (or knowledge-able about competing prices) if they are buying Victoria's Secret products as gifts for women. On the other hand, attracting more women through reduced "ladies' night" drink prices is a gender-pricing technique that enhances the value for eligible men to patronize a bar. Singles bars capitalize on this increased value by charging men higher drink prices.

Sometimes a less obvious characteristic can prove effective, such as a customer's proximity to an attraction like an amusement park or a ski resort. Out-of-state patrons who spend thousands on travel and hotels usually value an attraction higher than do those living down the street. To benefit from these differences, Disneyland regularly offers lower prices to in-state residents who show proof of residency. Ski resorts in Colorado use a similar approach. For an annual fee of $299, skiers can purchase a Buddy Pass that provides unlimited skiing in Breckenridge, Keystone, and the Arapahoe Basin for the entire 2004/2005 season. This is a considerable savings over the $65 average daily lift-ticket price in these areas. While technically available to anyone (in-state as well as out-of-state skiers), the procedure for buying a Buddy Pass makes it impractical for tourists to purchase one. Sales typically begin in late summer and end well in advance of the beginning of the ski season. To further limit sales to in-state residents, customers must purchase their Buddy Pass in person (and have their picture taken at the same time) at one of a handful of Colorado locations. This pricing tactic offers two benefits to ski resorts. First, locals (who are presumed to have lower valuations) receive discounts. Second, the Buddy Pass stimulates additional purchases. If discounts are only offered on full-day tickets, locals will limit their visits to the occasions when they can take advantage of a full day of skiing. The benefit of unlimited skiing makes it possible for locals to ski for a few hours and purchase additional products (e.g., refreshments, a hotel room, a night out on the town, etc.). The "free" price of a few hours of skiing thus creates demand for related products.

Actions Speak Louder
Than Words—Hurdles

Why not just ask each customer directly what she is willing to pay for a product and charge her that amount? The problem with this, of course, is that the prospect of a discount can tempt even the most ethical person to tell a white lie: "I'm *really* not a fan of the lime-green color, but I'll take that couch off your hands for a hundred dollars." One way to identify price-sensitive customers is to let their actions speak louder than their words by using hurdles, which require customers to take a conscious action in order to receive a discount. Hurdles provide the opportunity for budget-minded customers to credibly proclaim, "Price is important to me."

Coupons are the most recognizable discount hurdle for thrifty customers. We're bombarded with them, so why doesn't everyone use them? Because it's a very laborious process to search for, clip, and redeem coupons. Only those who truly care about price make the effort to jump over these hurdles. A colleague of mine recently dropped by my office, excited, to let me know that a national book chain (with a nearby location) had a 10% off coupon in that morning's *New York Times*. While waiting in that bookstore's checkout line a few days later, I saw another customer redeem her 10% discount coupon and realized that I had left mine at home. I started wondering why I had, in essence, thrown away a $5 bill (a 10% savings on my $50 purchase) by not bringing the coupon. I concluded that the reason for my forgetfulness was that the savings were not meaningful to me. Now, had the discount been 50%, I probably would have remembered. My friend, on the other hand, took full advantage of the discount. "Rafi, you can buy as many items as you want and get ten percent off of everything," he exclaimed with glee when I later saw him carrying two overstuffed bags of books. This is the wonderful benefit of offering coupons: only those who really value the discount actually use them.

Hurdles are also the reason department stores periodically offer special 10% early-bird discounts to those who shop between six A.M. and nine A.M. on a Sunday morning. Who is out shopping at six A.M. on this traditional day of rest? *Customers who care about price.* This early-morning hurdle is a good way to distinguish customers who are more likely to buy at a lower price. Similarly, some luxury furniture stores openly tell customers about their annual "customer-appreciation sale," which occurs every year during the third weekend of February. Who waits until the third weekend of February to buy furniture? *Customers who care about price.* Some retailers offer a discount to those who bring in a used product. A local men's-fashion retailer recently ran a promotion offering a $100 credit toward a suit priced at $399 or more to those who brought in an old suit. Curious, I asked a salesperson what they did with the used suits. He responded, "We donate them to charity." Who makes the effort to bring an old suit to the store? *Customers who care about price.*

Membership in clubs like Sam's or the American Automobile Association (AAA) usually reveals that a customer is price-sensitive. Many companies, not related to these clubs, offer discounts to customers who show their membership cards. A membership card is a badge that says, "I care about price." Customers who pay $25 to $30 a year for an Entertainment Book go one step further in pledging their allegiance to discounts. (An Entertainment Book is a thick compilation of hundreds of coupons good at local and national business establishments. Companies that include coupons in the Entertainment Book can be confident that their discounts are being targeted toward thrifty customers.)

Size can also be used as a hurdle to serve price-sensitive customers. Remember my purchase of thirty-two pounds of powdered laundry detergent in Chapter 4? It wasn't easy to lug that two-year supply of detergent into my condominium, and the large container now dominates my small laundry room. The inconvenience and additional upfront expenditure of buying large sizes can be a hurdle to sell only to customers who care about price.

The threat of not buying a product is often viewed as a credible hurdle to qualify for a discount. Have you tried to cancel a credit card lately? Once you state your desire to cancel, the wheeling and dealing begins. You are transferred to a "cancellation specialist" whose sole job is to find the weak spot that will change your mind. A lower interest rate? Five thousand frequent-flier miles? A 20% discount on the annual fee? These offers are last-ditch efforts to find the right price to keep customers.

Sometimes the hurdle to a discount is simply the ability to ask for one. I used to travel frequently between Boston and Los Angeles. Delta Airlines entered the transcontinental market with two-class aircraft seating, featuring standard coach and a new BusinessElite service. Intrigued by BusinessElite's pledge of five feet of legroom and the opportunity to recline almost horizontally, I called to inquire about prices. The reservationist quoted a round-trip price of $3,514. After a bit of sticker-shocked grousing, I inquired if there was a lower price. The reservationist asked if I was in Delta's frequent-flier program (free to join, no minimum mileage requirement). When I replied that I was, she quoted a price of $2,440 (same service, same restrictions as the $3,514 ticket). By just asking, I saved more than $1,000 and received a price that was lower than the full-fare coach price.

Time

Many new products initially carry a premium price to capitalize on customers who highly value the item and the bragging rights of being among the first in their neighborhood to own the latest gadget. Over time, prices are dropped to sell to more price-sensitive customers. For example, when Palm Pilots were introduced in 1996, they were priced at over $500. Today, some Palm Pilot models can be had for as little as $70. Time successfully distinguished customers with different valuations and allowed Palm to maximize the profits from its innovative product. The fashion industry uses the same technique. To capitalize on those who value being the first to wear the latest styles, prices are set high at the beginning of a season. As the season progresses, prices are lowered to attract customers who still value wearing the apparel for the remaining (less-than-full) season. Customers who have to have it now are really saying, "I value the product highly." In contrast, customers with lower valuations will patiently wait for a sale. Publishers also use the time between publishing hardcover and paperback books to segment value. Those willing to wait to purchase the paperback edition are rewarded with a 30% to 40% discount off the hardcover price.

Stores that sell popular new CDs and books often take a contrary pricing approach. Often, hordes of fans line up at midnight to purchase their favorite band's new release or the latest *Harry Potter* book. These customers are all but screaming, "Charge me more!" But instead of doing so, music and book retailers initially set low prices (sometimes below cost) and gradually raise them over time. What's going on here? Companies like Best Buy opt to use low prices to draw customers into the store. They hope that the profits missed from the new-release product will be more than made up for by other product purchases. This seems reasonable. Okay, so why don't music and book companies increase the wholesale price of their products sold during the first week of release? I recently asked this very question to several executives in both industries. While they were concerned that retailers would resist such a practice, most focused more on the importance of a new CD or book being listed as a bestseller on a top-ten sales list (e.g., *Billboard* for music, the *New York Times* for books). This list is important from a marketing standpoint—there is added value to being a popular product—and music artists and authors personally value a high ranking. Executives do not want to risk the possibility that an increased price will cause their new product to not "chart well." So while both producers (music companies, book publishers) and retailers (e.g., Wal-Mart) could set new-release prices higher, they choose instead to monetize the enhanced value through marketing benefits.

Sometimes early purchases do not account for value that occurs at a later date. Tickets purchased in January for a Red Sox game in August (seven months later) do not reflect the increased value that is created if the team is in a pennant race. Most events (e.g., sports or music) start selling tickets months before the date of performance. Given the long sales window, a last-minute purchase usually indicates that some additional, often impulsive, value triggered interest (e.g., it's a beautiful night for a concert at an outdoor amphitheater). Events try to capture this added value by charging higher day-of-the-show prices. In the case of the New York Yankees, a $5 premium is added to each ticket sold on the day of a game.

Quantity Discounts

The notion of "If you buy more, we'll offer a lower per-unit price" is firmly ingrained in our marketplace. While there are several reasons to offer volume discounts, some businesses axiomatically hand out discounts without questioning their necessity. Better understanding the rationale for volume discounts provides an opportunity to further uncover your product's hidden profits.

Think about your last trip to the movies. For many of us, the enticing price of a jumbo-sized bucket of popcorn is too attractive to pass up. The first few handfuls always taste great, but reaching deeper into the bucket, you value each additional scoop of popcorn less. Why? The more we consume, the less we value an additional unit of a product. This experience is another fundamental principle of economics: the law of diminishing returns. An important reason to offer volume discounts is to capitalize on the law of diminishing returns. Lower prices are a time-honored incentive to persuade customers to consume more.

The convenience-store chain 7-Eleven does an excellent job of incorporating the law of diminishing returns into the pricing of its fountain drinks. The chain sells soda in sizes that range from "small" twelve-ounce cups to monstrous fifty-two-ounce X-treme Gulp mugs. The relatively small price difference between cup sizes, especially between the larger volumes, causes some customers to reason, "For only an additional twenty cents, I get a third more!" Given the low cost of soda, even a small price difference (relative to a large increase in cup size) provides more profit. Similarly, quantity promotions like "buy one get one for 50% off" benefit from the idea that additional products are valued at lower prices. The "50% off" wording is also more attention-grabbing than the actual 25% effective discount on each product.

Volume discounts can also be used to reward customers' loyalty—or perhaps to bribe them into being loyal. Barnes & Noble offers a membership program that provides discounts to customers willing to back up their claim that they *will be* a high-volume buyer with a monetary pledge. For an annual fee of $25, members receive a 5% to 10% discount on all purchases. To cost-justify a membership, members must anticipate spending $250 to $500 during the year. Once customers have pledged $25, the draw of a discount can keep them from patronizing rival booksellers. Similar types of volume discounts have promotional value. I must confess that just having a Coffee Bean promotion card (buy nine coffees, get the tenth for free) in my wallet influences my decision about where to purchase my morning lattes whenever I'm in Los Angeles.

As you can see, there are many justifications for quantity discounts. My only caution is that you should understand *why* you are granting a discount. Sometimes large orders simply mean, "I love your product." On the way to a barbecue last summer, I stopped by my local gourmet food shop to buy thirty pounds of beef ribs to make my famous Korean-style ribs. The butcher's brightened mood, brought about by a seemingly quick and profitable sale, dampened when I asked him to cut the ribs thinly. After twenty minutes of intense slicing (and several reminders to "cut it thinner"), the meat was ornately packaged and ready to go. As you probably guessed, I could not resist the temptation of inquiring: "Since I am buying a lot of meat, do I get a volume discount?" Even I was surprised when the butcher, literally without a second thought, sliced the price from $8 to $6 a pound. While I appreciated the $60 savings, there really was no reason for him to offer the discount; I had not indicated that price was an issue and had already made the order at the agreed-upon price.

Distribution

Firms often charge different prices for the same merchandise based on where customers make purchases. *Where* customers shop is a good indicator of *how* they value product. I recently visited Brooks Brothers' stylish store on Rodeo Drive and was impressed by the beauty of the store, the high level of service, and the fact that most items were selling at full price (the salesman quickly moved on after I inquired where the sale rack was located). What struck me most was how well the store was doing; customers were leaving with bulging bags of clothes. Of course, I left empty-handed. Thrifty consumers like me often forgo the convenience of purchasing at Brooks Brothers retail stores and instead travel to its outlet stores to buy the same merchandise at a 30% to 50% discount.

The airline industry is adept at using distribution points to charge different prices for the same product. Airlines charge different prices depending on whether customers call their reservations centers or use their websites. They also offer specially negotiated prices to large travel agencies and high-volume websites like Travelocity. Customers can also roll the dice on their airline tickets by using websites like Hotwire.

While providing considerable savings, the drawback of using Hotwire is that your itinerary (as well as the airline) is revealed only *after* your credit card is charged (nonrefundable). Finally, many airlines use consolidators (sometimes called "bucket shops") to sell tickets. Consolidators purchase inventory in bulk and resell the inventory to individuals. These resellers typically have small ads in the Sunday travel sections of major newspapers, offering low prices to international destinations. While in the past consolidators tended to sell tickets only on lower-quality airlines (trust me, cramming in a few extra rows of seats and having only two working restrooms can *really* make a trip miserable), today virtually all top airlines sell tickets through consolidators. I regularly use consolidators to book my trips to Europe. After saving at least 20% on a ticket, I always wonder in amazement, "Why doesn't everyone use consolidators to purchase their international tickets?" The answer, of course, is that not everyone cares about price.

Many luxury brands use outlet stores to sell slow-moving merchandise. Luxury brands, such as Prada, profit from their high-end images. These prestigious retailers fear that offering discounts at their fashionable boutiques will cheapen their carefully crafted reputations. One brand-saving alternative is to sell discounted merchandise at outlets that are usually located sixty miles or more from an urban area.[57] In addition to the long drive, a major drawback of outlet-store shopping is that there is no guarantee that popular products will be in stock. Thus, discount-seeking urbanites risk the possibility of making a long drive only to be disappointed with a less-than-appealing inventory selection. This effectively separates big spenders from those who are willing to buy name brands only if the price is right.

Many manufacturers differentially price by geographic locations. It makes sense to set prices that reflect how a product is valued in different regions. One note of caution, though: if the price differences become too great, it may be financially advantageous for retailers to import items from lower-priced areas. This is what exactly happened to Levi Strauss. Tesco, one of Britain's leading retailers, stopped purchasing Levi's jeans from high-priced British wholesalers and started importing lower-priced jeans directly from the United States. This allowed Tesco to set lower prices—£27.99 ($39)—compared to the £50 ($70) that was being charged at rival British department stores.[58] Obviously, geographic pricing will not succeed if all buyers use this arbitrage strategy (i.e., create a gray market by shunning local wholesalers in favor of importing products from areas where prices are lower). For example, the cellular-phone industry in India suffered such a fate. Because cellular handsets could be profitably imported from countries with lower prices, at one point 90% of all mobile phones in India were purchased on the gray market.[59]

There are steps that manufacturers can take to make gray-market products less attractive. Many electronics stores in New York's Times Square area directly import merchandise from overseas (from Singapore, for example). These imported items are usually identical to those sold in the United States. Because of lower costs, however, these retailers set prices that are as much as 50% below those of rivals selling merchandise bought from U.S. wholesalers. To limit gray-market sales, manufacturers restrict warranties to the regions where their products were shipped (identifiable by serial number). Thus, a product shipped to Singapore is eligible for warranty service only in that region. The lack of a U.S. warranty is usually a big enough barrier to dissuade customers from buying gray-market products.

Mixed Bundling

Mixed bundling is one of the most popular pricing practices used in business today. This tactic involves selling products individually as well as in discounted bundles (the bundle price is less than the sum of the individual component prices). Because mixed bundling is so easy to implement, many managers are deceived into thinking that it is straightforward and simple. It is a powerful pricing technique, but despite its widespread use, most businesses do not understand how to fully utilize the capabilities of mixed bundling to uncover their hidden profits.

My editor, John, is always game for a challenging discussion. The other day at lunch, I bet him the check that I could show him how to make more money by using mixed bundling. After he skeptically agreed, I called the waiter over to change my order from a turkey sandwich to a large lobster with crab-meat stuffing—John's a nice guy, but if he wants to play the equivalent of three-card monte with me, I'm happy to let him buy me lunch.

John recently mentored two bestselling books by Larry Bossidy and Ram Charan: *Execution* and *Confronting Reality*.

Execution provides managers with the tools to get the job done and deliver results and has been a bestseller since its publication in 2002. The authors' follow-up book, *Confronting Reality,* shows managers how to profit from realistically and rigorously examining every facet of their businesses. Each book is priced at $27.50. Thus, customers will only purchase a copy if they value it at or above $27.50.

I suggested that in addition to selling the books individually, John should offer a bundle that contains both *Execution* and *Confronting Reality* for $50. This bundle would have the following differential-pricing effects:

Incentive to Buy More. Like many of you, I've succumbed to the pricing charms of a discounted bundle. The discount associated with a bundle often makes a deal too good to pass up. In this case, customers about to pay $27.50 for *Execution* may be persuaded to buy the bundle because in essence, they are paying a lower price of $22.50 for *Confronting Reality.* This discount serves as an incentive for customers to buy products that they otherwise would not purchase. From a differential-pricing standpoint, customers buying the bundle pay less per book compared to those making individual purchases.[60]

Attract a Wider Spectrum of Customers. A bundle price offers the flexibility to sell to customers with widely varying valuations. In this case, the $50 bundle price attracts readers with a $23: *Execution,* $27: *Confronting Reality* valuation, as well as those with valuations of ($24, $26); ($25, $26); ($27, $23); ($28, $23); etc. As you can see, customers who purchase bundles often implicitly pay different prices for the same book. This flexibility in accommodating customers' valuations allows mixed bundling to capitalize on lessons from an auction.[61]

As he was paying the bill, John winked and told me one of the oldest jokes in publishing: "Don't worry, I'll deduct the cost of this lunch from your royalties." Authors rarely find this joke to be as humorous as editors do.

Negotiation

Whenever possible, the easiest way to differential price is to negotiate with each customer individually. The problem is that this isn't practical for most products. It's impossible to negotiate individually with each customer waiting in line at the cash register. Customers are also unlikely to pay higher prices if they see that the person ahead of them in line was charged a lower amount. There are, however, many products, such as cars, where it is customary to negotiate price. In these negotiating situations, you know that other customers are paying different prices. Of course, the goal of a good salesperson is to make us feel like we got the best possible deal. Skilled negotiators use basic information to provide clues to a customer's willingness to pay. So, the next time a construction contractor stops by your house to give you an estimate, park the expensive European cars down the street, wear old blue jeans, and temper your enthusiasm about starting the project.

I once worked with a high-margin directory provider on its pricing strategy. It was in essence the yellow pages for a lucrative services industry. This directory was so highly regarded that if a firm did not advertise its capabilities and key personnel in the directory, the quality of the firm would be questioned. Additionally, most employees felt it important and a sign of prestige to be listed in this directory. Because customers were starting to use the Internet to search for the information contained in the directory, the company was facing classic commoditization pricing pressures. The directory provider had two important reasons for using a multi-price mindset. First, this selling technique resulted in the most sales, so profits from directory listings were maximized. But just as important, customers who paid thousands of dollars to buy the directory valued a comprehensive listing of sellers. If the industry's big names were not listed, the directory's value lost its luster. Thus, the directory had an extra incentive to price in a manner that attracted as many listings as possible. After a morning of discussing pricing with the sales force, it quickly became clear that some customers valued being listed in the directory more than others did. In fact, it was easy to use readily identifiable characteristics to identify companies with different listing valuations. The solution was simple; we created a scorecard using characteristics like firm size, geographic location, and types of business specialties that the sales force could use in their individual negotiations to instantly get an idea of each company's willingness to pay. For example, we discovered that second-tier firms in the Midwest valued a listing more than did top-rated New York firms.

Because of my interest in pricing, many friends ask me to accompany them to negotiate the price when they purchase a new car. It's fun for me. I enjoy saving them money and am fascinated by the sales process. We always get (or at least think we get) a great deal. There are two keys to my negotiating success. First, I always go to the showroom close to the end of the month (the end of a sales-quota cycle) during slow buying months (e.g., January, a time when consumers have spent their money on the holidays), when salespeople are motivated to make a deal. Second, my negotiation style is based on the crowd-pleasing antics of soul singer James Brown's famous cape routine. At the end of every performance, the Godfather of Soul goes through a routine where he acts exhausted from the performance, has his assistant put on his cape, and then pretends to leave. As the enthusiastic crowd screams their desire for more, he throws down the cape and comes back to sing another classic hit. He often does the routine several times before ending a concert. Much like Mr. Brown, I always perform a similar routine: I put on my cape (it's surprisingly fashionable), pretend to leave the showroom, and am usually brought back to the negotiating table by shouts . . . of a lower price.

CHAPTER 7

Versioning

Follow the Food

The key to solving most crimes is to "follow the money." That's what Deep Throat told Woodward and Bernstein when they investigated Watergate, ultimately leading to the resignation of President Nixon. It's also led to the downfall of seemingly untouchable gangsters, as well as once-admired Fortune 500 companies. Similarly, the secret to finding budget-challenged graduate students at any major university is to "follow the food." The promise of an after-seminar reception of free drinks and appetizers compelled me and my classmates to endure ninety-minute presentations on complex economics papers that contained more mathematical equations than written words. The same held true for our local bars and restaurants . . . ten-cent chicken wings on Tuesdays at four? We were there. We were broke.

Mr. Kapoor, the owner of the Maharaja Palace Indian restaurant in Collegetown, visibly shuddered whenever we appeared at his $4 lunch buffet. Amid our unrelenting demands for "more bread," he helplessly watched his profit margins literally being eaten away. "It'll take twenty minutes to replenish some of the buffet dishes? No problem. Can we have another free refill of hot tea?" We had all afternoon to hang out at his restaurant (there are few classes or responsibilities in graduate school). Once, after watching a classmate devour eight pieces of tandoori chicken, I could not resist commenting, "Do you realize that you just ate an entire chicken?" His response? "More bread."

But when we came for dinner, Mr. Kapoor looked less annoyed. His dinnertime pricing strategy guaranteed that he would eke at least a small profit out of us. I had learned about versioning in my price-theory class, but it was only after observing how the other customers in the restaurant ordered that I truly understood the concept. Since diners typically order entrées, most restaurants price entrées with low margins. This makes the restaurant accessible to customers with a wide range of valuations. The real profits come from the other products sold by the restaurant, so appetizers, side dishes, drinks, wine, and desserts are loaded with higher margins.

We were content dining on entrées (low-margin) and tea (refills were still free at night). Richer "townies" sitting next to us also ordered appetizers and desserts (higher margins). Professors in sport coats sipped glasses of wine (premium margins). Back in the private-function room, a New York City investment bank wined and dined prospective recruits with an open bar and a sumptuous, multicourse "Maharaja" dinner (super margins). This was the key to versioning, I realized: offer your customers a range of products and accompanying prices (with different margins). Then allow them to choose the products that match their value. Customers reveal their valuations in the way they order.

Versioning is a multi-price mindset strategy that involves selling *similar* products to *different* customers at *different* prices. This strategy involves offering a series of products at different prices, generally based on a core product. Services and products are typically versioned by offering good, better, and best options. Customers then purchase the option that best fits their valuation. In the case of the Maharaja Palace, customers create their own customized version of an Indian dinner that reflects the value they place on dining at the restaurant.

Many managers fear that if they offer a low-priced, stripped-down model, everyone will just buy the basic product. That's not necessarily true; *even I* buy premium gas some of the time. Some customers value higher-quality products (better-constructed, respected brand names), as well as those with added bells and whistles (extra attributes). Still don't believe me? Drop by your local Hugo Boss, Williams-Sonoma, or Pottery Barn store and check out the fancy products customers with high valuations are buying. Down the street at Kmart, you'll find customers with lower valuations purchasing similar products that have fewer attributes or are lower in quality. Customers will purchase the version that best fits their valuation.

Versioning allows companies to enhance profits in two key

ways. First, in line with the goal of the multi-price mindset, versioning capitalizes on different customer valuations. Those with high valuations are usually less inclined to evaluate the trade-offs between different versions and their respective prices. They just buy the most expensive version. Similarly, high-income customers who "have to have the best" rarely consider lower-priced models. Versioning also sells to customers with lower valuations. To serve these customers, many electronics manufacturers sell "factory-refurbished" merchandise. These gadgets, which were returned to the manufacturer because of a small defect or a customer's changed mind, have been restored to "almost-new" condition. Thrifty customers who can bear knowing that someone else previously used their product can buy refurbished merchandise for 30% to 40% below the "brand-new" price.

Second, and just as important, adding attributes to a product can attract new customers. Diet Coke, introduced in 1982, is a version of the classic Coca-Cola drink that was developed close to one hundred years earlier. Using similar manufacturing, marketing, and distribution processes, this versioned product is targeted toward weight-conscious consumers. Because of its success in attracting these new customers, Diet Coke is now the number-one sugar-free drink in the United States, as well as the number-three soft drink in the world.

Versioning is also cost-effective. The great thing about versioning is that most of the costs associated with this strategy have already been incurred. The big investment was developing the core product. A few relatively low-cost subsequent investments can allow you to tweak your product in a manner that increases your profits and broadens your customer base. Admittedly, the costs to develop Diet Coke were high, but certainly not as much as if it had been created from scratch. Diet Coke has since been versioned (at much lower costs) to offer a line of caffeine-free, vanilla, lemon, cherry, lime, and Splenda-sweetened drinks.

This chapter provides a comprehensive set of versioning approaches that can transform your product in order for you to effectively price for profits and growth. In the rest of the chapter, I'm going to outline for you a way to "follow the value" to an effective versioning strategy. There are seven techniques to version your product:

1. A La Carte. Can you offer customers a menu of options to version your product?

2. More is Better. Can you offer products with "more" (e.g., higher quantity, quality, support, or experience) to generate higher margins and/or new customers?

3. Less Can Be Profitable. Can you offer "less" (e.g., lower quantity, quality, service, or experience) to attract new (usually value-conscious) customers?

4. Add or Subtract Features. Can you change your product's attributes in a manner that will attract new customers?

5. Expedited Service. Can you provide faster service to your customers?

6. Avoid the Wait. Can you offer options that allow customers to go to the head of the line?

7. Uncertainty. Can different levels of uncertainty (i.e., reducing consumer risk or your risk) be used to version your product?

A La Carte

One of the simplest versioning techniques is to offer several options and allow customers to build the product or experience that best satisfies their valuations. Cruise lines like Holland America are expert at using a la carte versioning. Once you've decided to take a cruise, you have a wealth of options to decide on: size and type of stateroom, cancellation insurance, excursions while in port, drinks, and the opportunity to dine at premium restaurants for a surcharge. Thus, for any cruise, the a la carte selections made by a customer can easily translate into a 50% price difference between a basic and a highly accessorized cruise.

A common misstep many companies make is focusing too intently on their core product, at the expense of earning additional profits from tangential products or services. A home-entertainment store may be known as the best place to shop for top-of-the line stereos and televisions. But if the retailer does not offer customers a la carte options like delivery, twenty-four-hour repair service, gift wrapping, and home-entertainment

149

design consultation, it misses the opportunity to bank additional profits from high-value customers. Even selling commonly available products like the latest music CDs, entertainment-center cabinets, and extra connection cords results in better margins. Don't waste the opportunity to let customers pay you more money. Offering the best product will bring customers in the door; selling a la carte options will send you and your family to the Cayman Islands.

More Is Better

Similar to the a la carte approach, the most popular form of versioning is based on the concept that "more is better." The idea is to build higher profit margins into products with "more" and sell this enhanced merchandise to customers who are less sensitive to price. For example, legions of loyal J.R.R. Tolkien fans enjoyed the *Lord of the Rings* trilogy of films at their local movie theaters. When it came time to purchase the DVDs, New Line Cinema (the studio that made the trilogy) used a more-is-better approach to capture different margins from different customers. For instance, customers shopping for *The Return of the King* (the last *Lord of the Rings* film) have three options: the two-disc regular DVD ($29.98) includes the film, as well as several extended scenes; the four-disc Platinum Series Special Extended Edition ($39.98) includes the film, as well as documentaries on how the film was made and fifty minutes of never-before-seen footage; and the five-disc Platinum Series Special Extended Edition Collector's Gift Set ($79.92) offers the film, more documentaries (including one that describes how the music to the movie was arranged), and a collectible polystone sculpture/keepsake box. These options allow customers to select the product that best fits how they value the home-entertainment DVD.

The key to more-is-better versioning is offering options to meet the needs of new customers. To serve customers with different quality needs, Sears offers both WeatherHandler ($59.99: eighteen-month warranty) and Gold ($79.99: thirty-six-month full replacement warranty) models of its well-known Diehard auto battery. MediSoft, a medical-billing software company, allows customers to choose the level of training and support that best suits them. Depending on their preferences, buyers choose between CD ($79 to $349), Web-based ($210), or video ($279) training. Additionally, the software company offers a year of unlimited telephone support for $799, or help can be bought by the hour (minimum ten-minute increments) for $129. Similarly, to appeal to well-heeled art lovers, New York's Museum of Modern Art offers the enhanced experience of touring the museum during times when it is closed to the general public.[62] This privilege, once limited to museum trustees, is now available for purchase on select Mondays for $50.

Less Can Be Profitable

While versioning often means adding more options so higher prices can be charged, Barnes & Noble is taking the opposite approach for certain types of books. Reasoning that some thrifty readers are willing to trade fancy covers for lower prices, the retailer is publishing a discounted "Classics" line of popular books. The savings from purchasing this private-label brand can be considerable. For instance, its Classics version of *The Scarlet Letter* is priced at $3.95, compared to the similar $6 paperback and $13.60 hardback editions the company also sells. Barnes & Noble plans to employ this stripped-down versioning technique to other types of popular books such as atlases, technology guides, and how-to guides. By 2008, the company hopes that its private-label titles will account for 10% to 12% of its total revenue.[63]

The ultimate approach to low-price versioning is to become a wholesaler and allow others to resell your product under their brand names. Sprint PCS operates as both a retailer and a wholesaler of cellular telephone service. In addition to selling its own branded cellular service, the company has resale agreements with cable companies (e.g., Time Warner), telecommunications companies (e.g., AT&T and Qwest), and new entrants (e.g., Virgin Mobile).[64] As a wholesaler, Sprint sells its service at a discount (relative to its retail price), and the buyers handle the rest of the business (e.g., marketing, creating new accounts, billing). In most cases, customers who purchase from these resellers do not know that they are using Sprint's service. These agreements allow Sprint to reach customers it would not otherwise reach. For example, the latest trend in communications is to offer one-stop-shopping bundles (e.g., local, long-distance, cellular, television, and Internet services). Since Sprint does not offer all these products, it makes sense to wholesale its service to companies that can sell such packages. This way, Sprint can earn some profit from customers wedded to purchasing a comprehensive package. Similarly, instead of creating a new brand to attract target-market teenagers, Sprint decided that it was easier to enter the prepaid teenage cellular market by reselling through an established, stylish brand— Virgin Mobile.

Features Attract New Customers

Versioning can also be used to attract customers who currently are not purchasing your product. The technique of horizontal versioning adds attributes to your product and can be the tipping point that motivates customers to purchase. A horizontally versioned product is not necessarily "better"; it just has more features. Apple is horizontally versioning its iPod music player. With current sales that are greater than all of its competitors' combined, Steve Jobs recently pronounced the iPod to be the "Walkman of the twenty-first century." Not content to rest on its laurels, Apple is adding features to draw in new customers. For instance, it recently introduced a red and black U2 iPod. Aside from the color, the endorsement of the rock band

U2, and a coupon offering a discount on the band's 446-song digital box set, this $349 model is identical to a white iPod model that sells for $299. While some may question whether the new attributes justify the $50 premium, customers are buying it. Apple also introduced an iPod Photo model that, in addition to playing music, allows owners to share and display photographs. The production cost of adding this feature to an identical music-only player is less than $20, but Apple charges $100 more for the iPod Photo.[65]

Ford's Lincoln division used a similar type of horizontal versioning on its Lincoln Navigator SUV. In August 2003, Lincoln rolled out a limited-edition Sean John Navigator that was designed by hip-hop mogul Sean "P. Diddy" Combs. Priced at $85,000—about $30,000 more than the SUV's normal sticker price—this enhanced Navigator offered such amenities as three DVD players, six television screens, a Sony PlayStation 2, and heated/vibrating front seats. Reinforcing the power of horizontal versioning to attract new customers, a Lincoln spokesman explained that the Sean John Navigator is "an extension of the brand" into markets where buyers might otherwise overlook the Navigator.[66]

Service can also be used to horizontally version a product. To attract new customers, the discount electronics retail chain Best Buy offers the option of paying for full service. Each of its stores has a Geek Squad staff. These technicians, clad in black clip-on ties, offer in-home electronics repair and installation. Their services range from $100 to debug a computer to $300 to set up a flat-panel television.[67] As is the case with Medi-Soft, Best Buy also vertically versions its service by offering lower prices to those who are willing to bring their electronics to a store. Running antivirus software on a PC in the store runs $40, while the same service at home costs $160. In an era where electronics are adding capabilities that require sophisticated programming, the option of this enhanced service makes purchasing from Best Buy especially attractive to technology-challenged customers (like me).

The key to horizontal versioning is to offer attributes that tweak a product to meet the needs of new customers. For example, to accommodate the differing lifestyles of its customers, Crunch Fitness offers plans that allow members to work out either at a designated health club or, for a higher fee, at any of its (or its affiliated) clubs across North America. Horizontal versioning is a staple for consumer-product companies. To better serve customers who value garnishing their hot dogs and hamburgers with pickles, for instance, manufacturers sell hamburger-chip slices and relish. I bet you didn't know that the real profits in the pickle industry come from these versioned cut items, not from whole pickle sales (I certainly didn't).[68]

Expedited Service

Customers are often willing to pay more for rush service. Depending on the guaranteed time of delivery, Federal Express customers pay between $17.81 (three-thirty P.M. guarantee) and $46.48 (eight-thirty A.M. guarantee) for overnight delivery of an eight-ounce envelope from New York to Los Angeles. Not everyone can offer this kind of rush service. For those who can, offering quicker service can be as easy as moving a customer's name up on the list or moving their dry cleaning to the top of the pile. Usually, though, it's more complex than that. Yet many companies still find that the costs incurred in reconfiguring their operations are small relative to the premium customers are willing to pay for faster service.

For example, the Union Pacific Railroad reconfigured its operations to offer shippers the option of purchasing expedited Blue Streak rail service. The company discovered that the cost of providing this priority service is only slightly higher than the cost of its normal service. This option makes Union Pacific's freight service competitive with trucking services (e.g., guaranteeing five-day service between Atlanta and Los Angeles). Demand was so strong that virtually all of the Blue Streak's capacity was sold out during its first year of operation. Since Blue Streak service commands up to a 40% premium, this new service, based on value, has been highly profitable for Union Pacific.

Avoid the Wait

The state of Washington has a wonderful array of rustic islands. One haven, Orcas Island, is reachable only by a one-hour trip on a ferry that leaves the mainland every three hours. One downside of making this trip, especially on busy weekends, is the ferry's policy of boarding cars on a first come, first served basis. This results in cars lining up hours before a departure. During popular periods, it is not uncommon for a ferry's capacity to be sold out hours before the ferry is to depart. This is a good example of how simply asking customers what they like and dislike about a product can offer insight into creating new value. If queried, I am sure that the wait time and risk associated with the first come, first served policy would be at the top of the negatives list. More profits would result from allocating at least a small percentage of the capacity for reservations and charging a significantly higher price for this newly minted value. It's not a stretch to imagine that more affluent customers may be willing to pay double the normal round-trip price of $37.50 for the security and time savings of a confirmed reservation.

For most of us, the prospect of visiting an amusement park is marred by the thought of waiting in long lines that snake back and forth. Many amusement parks now offer an option that allows customers to go to the head of the line. At Universal Studios Hollywood, an $89.75 "magical" necklace (a $40 premium over the regular admission price) allows well-heeled visitors to enter rides through a separate entrance that merges them with regular visitors at the front of the line. Legoland in California offers a similar $100 VIP wristband (regular admission price: $43.95). Worried that some of its younger guests might spot the line-cutters and cry, VIPs enter rides via the regular exit.[69] This makes the line-jumpers less visible to those sweltering at the end of the line. This VIP treatment pads the bottom line in two important ways. Some current customers will trade up to this higher-margin experience. In addition, just as important, this option may attract a new segment of customers. Customers who had previously refrained from visiting the park because of long lines may now be drawn to the privileges of being a VIP.

Uncertainty

In many industries, buyers and sellers face a variety of risks. For example, buyers often face uncertainty in securing a steady supply of inputs at a fixed price. Others face uncertainty in knowing what their future needs will be and value the option to make last-minute purchases (e.g., business travelers often pay ten times more for an airline ticket than leisure passengers because they value the options to make last-minute bookings, changes, or cancellations). Sellers also face risk. Many businesses make sizable investments to create new products and face uncertainty about how they will be accepted by the market. Products can be versioned to profitably share these types of risks. Offering uncertainty-based product versions can increase your profits (customers pay for peace of mind), increase your customer base (customers are drawn to a product that fits their risk profile), and make your business run better (share risk with customers).

Customers often face uncertainty about critical inputs, in terms of both securing a steady supply and the price that they will have to pay. Many are willing to pay an insurance premium to mitigate these risks. For instance, beef wholesalers usually offer high-volume customers (restaurants and retailers) the option to lock into set prices through forward twelve-month contracts. These contracts offer protection against the price instability that is common in the beef market. For instance, demand for beef seems to change every few months. If the meat-loving Atkins is the "in" diet, beef is a hot commodity. However, if the low fat South Beach Diet is "in," beef falls out of favor. Similarly, the beef supply depends on many factors, including ranchers' decisions about how much cattle to raise, weather conditions, and recently, concerns over mad cow disease (the United States bans beef imported from countries where cattle have been infected with this malady). As a result of the volatility in both demand and supply, meat prices constantly vary. For example, in one month alone (October 2003) beef prices rose by 40%. These cost swings wreak havoc on restaurants' and retailers' profit margins. They often struggle in deciding what portion can be passed on to consumers and how much they will have to "eat," so to speak. Customers who value having peace of mind over critical input costs buy forward contracts.

Versioning can also reduce sellers' risks. Many châteaus in Bordeaux use wine futures to share risk with customers and improve their cash flow. These châteaus are often cash-flow challenged because there is usually a two-year lag between when a wine is made and when it's available for sale at retailers. In addition, until it hits the market (and critics have rated it), châteaus don't know the value of their wines. Futures contracts help manage both of these issues. The futures process works in the following manner. Shortly after the wine is fermented (a few months after the fall grape harvest), select critics are allowed to taste the fresh wine. Shortly thereafter, futures contracts are offered for wine that will be delivered in two years.[70] Customers buy wine futures based on the opinions of early tasters, the grape harvest conditions, and the châteaus' reputations. They hope that by purchasing futures now, they'll save money when the wine later hits retailers' shelves (presumably at higher prices). Because both buyers and sellers value their benefits, futures are becoming a popular pricing technique in the wine industry. For example, after the well-regarded 2000 Bordeaux vintage was released in June 2001, the San Francisco retailer The Wine Club sold $1 million worth of Bordeaux futures in one day, and $11 million worth of futures that year. Given that the retailer's total sales were $47 million, wine futures represented a significant component of its sales.[71]

Versioning can also help companies control their costs. Utilities use versioning to share risk with customers. Especially during hot summers, when energy-gulping air conditioners are set on high, utilities worry about demand overwhelming their fixed capacity. This strong demand can lead to a costly and disastrous energy blackout. Instead of building expensive, additional capacity that will be rarely—if ever—used to reduce the risk of this occurring, utilities version their products to share risk with large-volume customers (e.g., manufacturers, large businesses). In exchange for lower energy prices, these customers agree to curtail their demand when energy prices drastically spike or excessive demand threatens to overload the network.

Offering a line of uncertainty-based product versions can better and more profitably serve different customers. The network-television industry uses this approach by selling both up-front contract and scatter commercial airtime. Each May, television networks sell 75% to 85% of all of their advertising time slots for the upcoming fall and spring seasons.[72] These up-front contract sales provide advertisers with guaranteed prices and the lead time necessary to plan a comprehensive marketing campaign. The remaining 15% to 25% is purposely held back for spot-market scatter sales. This better serves customers who are forced by the nature of their businesses to make last-minute decisions. Movie studios, for example, do not map out a film's long-term advertising campaign in advance. It is only after the make-or-break first box-office weekend that studios can gauge a film's long-term commercial prospects. If the film performs well, studios want to buy same-week television advertising to further promote it. These customers are willing to pay higher prices for the flexibility of making last-minute decisions. As a result, scatter advertising often ends up being sold for a premium (as much as 50% more than the prices charged during the up-front sales period) or not generating any revenue (used to promote the network's shows).[73]

CHAPTER 8

Segment-Based Pricing

Graduate School, Rock and Roll, and Bundling Profits

My graduate-school classmates were not just hungry, they were also very socially conscious. They wanted to change the world—and some of them are succeeding. Their dissertations focused on public-policy ideas in heady areas like social-security reform, fostering economic growth in developing countries, and improving the U.S. welfare system. To support their new ideas, they traveled to out-of-the-way countries to meet political leaders, study their policies, and collect data. Their dedication was impressive. My research was a little less ambitious . . . in terms of changing the world, I mean. I wrote my dissertation on pricing and bundling strategies in the rock-concert industry. In the name of research (seeking important insights and data),

I felt it necessary to follow rock singer Jimmy Buffett across the United States on several of his summer concert tours. While no important public-policy makers or foreign dignitaries called me to discuss the public-policy uses of my scholarly pursuits, I did hear a lot of good music and had the opportunity to meet a number of nice and interesting people in the music business. I was interested in understanding how pricing strategies can attract new customers to a product, something every manager wants. Generating blockbuster growth can be as easy as adding a new pricing strategy.

Summer is the primary season for rock concerts. Most concerts are held at outdoor amphitheaters, with two types of seating: pavilion and lawn. Pavilion seats (closest to the stage; assigned seating; and a covered roof that protects the crowd from rain) are generally preferred to those on the lawn (no physical seats; spots on the lawn are first come, first served; and no rain protection). One drawback of going to concerts, of course, is that tickets to shows that everyone wants to see are always difficult to get. For the most popular concerts, you have to purchase tickets at the exact moment they go on sale, and the desirable pavilion seats sell out quickly.

To make the ticket-buying process easier, as well as to attract new customers, some amphitheaters use a subscription-series bundling tactic. With this new selling technique, tickets are initially sold only in bundles of four or five concerts. Individual tickets are not sold during this period, and subscription series are sold only through mail order. After tickets have been allocated to these bundle purchases, the remaining tickets are sold individually. Music fans like this selling technique because it's easy to order tickets, pavilion seats are pretty much guaranteed, and the best seats are reserved for those who purchase bundles. For me (as a researcher), this approach was interesting for two reasons. First, unlike with any bundling concept known to the business world, in this instance the bundle price was *greater* than the sum of the individual ticket prices (in contrast to the bundles I talked about earlier, where the bundle price was lower). This anomaly provided the opportunity to discuss a new pricing concept.

Second, approximately 33% of the major amphitheaters in the United States used this bundling approach. The rest sold tickets individually. Since the same acts played at each amphitheater, I had great experimental (selling subscription series) and control (individual sales) markets. This allowed me to statistically calculate how many additional tickets a band sold simply because they were included in a subscription series.

I discovered that bundling is very profitable and generates impressive growth. By just being included in the bundle, each "dog" act (less popular bands) sold an additional 3,187 tickets. Even the most popular bands sold an additional 724 tickets because they were in the bundle. Given that the average concert attendance was 11,585, this growth is significant. Where did all these new customers come from? First, some customers bought the bundle, which included tickets for some shows that they would otherwise not have seen, just for the security of having pavilion seats for their favorite concerts. Second, some bought the bundle because the mail-order process was so convenient to use. Implementing this pricing tactic resulted in higher ticket prices (bundles were priced as much as 20% above the sum of the individual ticket prices), 6% to 27.5% more tickets sold for each concert (the cost of accommodating additional fans is negligible), amphitheaters and bands selling additional products (refreshments, parking, CDs, T-shirts, etc.), and bands gaining valuable exposure to new fans. Not bad for a pricing concept that costs almost nothing to implement.

Segment-based pricing is a multi-price mindset strategy that activates dormant customers by employing new pricing strategies. Just like bundling does in the rock-concert industry, a new pricing concept can grow your customer base. What's great about this strategy is that it capitalizes on interest that currently exists for your product. You've invested a lot of money and energy to bring your product to market. In the process, you've generated a lot of customer interest. For some customers, the roadblock to making a purchase is the way that you price—it just doesn't work for them. In this chapter, I discuss ten different types of pricing techniques and show you how they can activate your dormant customers.

1. Interval Ownership. Can you attract new customers by subdividing your product into smaller increments?

2. Bundling. Can bundling be used to grow your customer base by promoting convenience or getting customers to purchase products they otherwise would not buy?

3. Leasing. Can the "trading up," convenience, and financing attributes of leasing draw new customers to your product?

4. Prepaid. Can the features of prepaid pricing (e.g., impose discipline, are easier to purchase, provide flexibility, serve the credit-challenged) attract new customers to your product?

5. Rental. Can you use rentals to serve new customers who want to use your product for a short period of time?

6. Two-Part Pricing. Can two-part pricing attract new customers by stimulating purchases and serving those with different valuations?

7. Hurdles. Can hurdles draw in new clients who use your service (and value it) differently than your current customers do?

8. Payment Plans. Can payment plans that better match customers' cash flows draw in new clients?

9. Customized. Can you use customized pricing to steal clients from rivals (who offer standard prices) as well as serve a new set of customers?

10. All-You-Can-Eat. Can the convenience and peace of mind provided by all-you-can-eat pricing attract new customers?

Interval Ownership

Interval ownership, the concept of dividing your product into smaller, more accessible parts, is one of the best examples of the explosive growth that can be created by a new pricing tactic. This pricing approach makes a product accessible to a new segment of customers. If you have spent any time in a resort area, you've undoubtedly been approached about attending a ninety-minute time-share (interval ownership) presentation in exchange for freebie tickets to a local attraction. These time-shares typically divide a condominium's usage into fifty-two-week segments. Customers purchase ownership for a week or two, good for the life of the condominium. This new pricing concept has made the American dream of owning a vacation house a reality for many people in the middle class, with handsome profits for the resort home–building industry.

Interval ownership has also revolutionized the private-jet industry. Because of the large financial commitment involved, private-jet ownership used to be limited to Fortune 500 companies and to the absolute wealthiest customers. A fully furnished Gulfstream V jet, for instance, can cost more than $40 million dollars. After making this major purchase, owners have to arrange maintenance and hire a crew. Interval ownership offers an alternative to these significant financial and organizational commitments. Instead of buying a jet outright, customers can purchase a fractional interest in a jet from companies like NetJets. For a quarter share of the aforementioned Gulfstream V, NetJets charges $10.1 million, a monthly fee of

$56,516, and $3,118 for each flight hour.[74] This quarter ownership provides one hundred flying hours (wheels-up to wheels-down) a year and the convenience of NetJets handling all of the staffing and maintenance requirements. Interval shares can be sold back to the company at any time for a price that reflects the aircraft's fair market value.

This pricing approach has opened the once ultra-exclusive world of private-jet ownership to a broader set of customers. Businesspeople, celebrities, and the merely (as opposed to the fabulously) wealthy can now affordably avoid long security lines, summon a jet with as little as four hours' notice, utilize five thousand U.S. airports (compared to the five hundred plus airports served by commercial airlines), fly in privacy, and travel nonstop on their own schedules. Billionaire Warren Buffett was so satisfied with his experience as a customer and so believed in the commercial potential of interval ownership that he bought the NetJets company in 1998.

The benefits that private-jet manufacturers have reaped from this new pricing structure are nothing short of impressive. Between 1995 and 2000, the interval-jet industry grew by 40% annually.[75] Private-jet sales have increased in lockstep with this newly created demand. Between 1996 and 2000, sales increased from close to $3 billion to almost $11 billion a year.[76] Even more astonishingly, sales to fractional jet companies now account for more than 75% of the order backlog of leading aircraft manufacturers like Cessna, Gulfstream, and Raytheon.[77] These statistics highlight the robust growth that can be created with new pricing concepts.

Bundling

A popular technique that attracts customers involves bundling products together (as I learned from my concert-tour research). One benefit of these bundles is the convenience they provide. In addition, some companies sell popular items only in bundles. This usually results in customers buying products that they otherwise would not purchase.

Returning to the interval-jet market, a key benefit of being a fractional owner is the convenience of the services bundled into the package. These services are the real motivation for many to become interval owners. Actor and politician Arnold Schwarzenegger used to own a private jet, but the associated headaches became too much. He complained: "You have pilots at your throat about vacation, that their wife is pregnant, why they can't have New Year's Eve off . . . it's on and on and on." Now, as an owner of several NetJets fractional interests, he is happy to let NetJets worry about managing the crew and handling all the other details. "I had to get over the ego thing. It's [not] my plane," he says, but "I like the package better."[78]

Selling bundles has also become the trend in financial services and telecommunications. Deregulation has led companies once limited to specific services to aspire to become one-stop providers. They are banking that customers will value the ease of handling all their transactions with a single company and the convenience of one monthly summary statement. For example, regional Bell phone companies that only offered local phone service before deregulation now offer bundles that include local, long-distance, wireless, and high-speed Internet services. Bundling has been a hit in the telecommunications industry. In 2004, 62% of households bought two or more services from the same company, up from 42% in 2002.[79] However, the pricing technique has been less successful for financial services. Citigroup, the financial giant that pioneered the one-stop financial-services shopping concept, sold its Travelers Life and Annuity insurance company in July 2005. The sale of this integral component of Citigroup's financial services bundle signals a shift away (and implicit acknowledgement of disappointing results) from the company's one-stop-shopping strategy. Switching costs play an important role in understanding why bundling has succeeded in telecommunications but failed in financial services. It's fairly easy to change your telecommunications provider. However, it requires far more effort to change financial service companies. A friend of mine put it best: "Rafi, I'd rather stick pins in my eyes than go through the hassle and paperwork of changing brokerage accounts." He's got a good point.

Popular items can be sold as part of a bundle as a means to get customers to purchase products they otherwise would not buy—to get the desired product, you have to buy the whole bundle. McDonald's used this tactic for its 1997 Teenie Beanie Baby promotion. At the time, full-sized Beanie Babies were the rage in the United States. With more than a hundred types of Beanie Babies on the market, McDonald's commissioned miniature (Teenie) versions of ten different characters to sell at its restaurants. The catch was that the only way to get a Teenie

Beanie Baby was to purchase a Happy Meal bundle that also included a hamburger, french fries, and a drink. Why not simply sell the dolls individually? Because then parents would just stop by the restaurant to buy the dolls. Bundling increased McDonald's sales in three key ways. First, more Happy Meals were sold to kids in the bundle's target market (children aged three to nine). Second, the parents who took the kids to McDonald's purchased other menu items. Finally, adults who wanted the Teenie Beanie Babies (there were many) bought Happy Meals. Sales surpassed every metric of success. Prior to this promotion, McDonald's was selling 10 million Happy Meals per week.[80] But when the Teenie Beanie Babies were added, close to 100 million Happy Meals were sold in ten days.[81]

Leasing

Leasing, purchasing the use of a product for a fixed period of time, has many attractive features that customers value. Payments are usually made monthly, and at the end of the lease term the product can be purchased at a previously agreed-upon price. Leasing was especially popular in the automobile industry in the '90s and peaked in 1999 with more than 3.7 million leasing transactions in the United States.[82]

One attraction of leasing is that in many cases, the upfront and monthly payments are lower than those of a financed sale. Since many customers think about their purchases in terms of their monthly payments, this allows them to trade up to a better (more profitable) product.

Leasing also offers convenience. Many customers prefer having a product that is covered by a full manufacturer's warranty. This protects them from large maintenance bills. Because most leases are for periods that are covered by the manufacturer's warranty, leasing is an attractive option for these customers. Similarly, many customers enjoy driving the latest car model. While they could purchase a car and resell it later, this can be a hassle. With leasing, you simply pick the car up and drop it off a few years later, when the lease is up.

Finally, leasing can be viewed as a valuable financing tool. Some buyers face a tight credit line, so if they finance a large purchase, their credit line is drawn down. One benefit of leasing is that while it usually requires similar monthly payments, it does not tap into a customer's credit line.

Leasing is also attractive to managers who want to avoid the purchasing bureaucracy in place at many large corporations. Most companies require tedious paperwork and approval from the guy in purchasing (who never seems to return phone calls) for big orders. Despite its being more expensive at times, many managers opt to lease a product (relatively small lease payments are usually below the "scrutiny" threshold) to avoid this laborious ordering process.

Prepaid

Prepaid pricing—customers paying in advance for a service and drawing down this credit with their usage—has unearthed large segments of new customers. This concept has been particularly successful in the telecommunications industry, which provides the clearest illustration of the attributes companies and customers find most valuable with this pricing approach. With most of the obvious customers now using cell phones, many wireless companies are using prepaid plans to draw new customers to fuel their rapid growth. These plans come with a fixed amount of minutes. After the minutes are used, the service shuts off; more minutes can be added by calling a toll-free number and paying by credit card. Some customers value the discipline that prepaid services impose on their usage. Cincinnati Bell's growth strategy focuses on offering prepaid pricing plans. They've succeeded, and now a third of the company's wireless customers are on prepaid plans.[83]

Prepaid pricing can make your product easier to purchase as well. Consider the long-distance market. Not too long ago, long-distance service was offered by the handful of firms—with their own sophisticated billing systems—who could afford to advertise heavily. Today, with the advent of prepaid calling cards, making a long-distance call is as easy as buying a card at your local 7-Eleven store. One interesting result of prepaid pricing is that since calling cards are so widely available, competition has pushed down prices. Some cards offer long-distance service for as little as two cents a minute. This is lower than what most people pay for their home long-distance service. So why doesn't everyone use prepaid cards to make long-distance phone calls? Some people are not willing to jump the low-price hurdle of calling a toll-free number, entering their card number, and then dialing the long-distance number. Others simply do not care about price.

Prepaid plans also offer flexibility. Wireless companies require customers to select a monthly plan that contains a set number of peak and off-peak minutes. Customers who do not use their full minutes allocation are in essence penalized (their actual realized per-minute price is higher). Conversely, because these companies usually set high prices for minutes used above their plan's limit (to encourage customers to trade up to more expensive, higher-minute plans), a high-usage month can result in super-sized additional charges. These plans are not well suited to customers with varying monthly usage. Since prepaid wireless plans are priced by the minute and typically do not have monthly minimums, they are ideal for these types of customers.

Finally, prepaid plans can serve customers with poor credit who are not able to purchase regular service. For example, some customers may not have a local phone line, or if they do, their service is restricted to local calls. Prepaid cards allow long-distance companies to profitably serve these customers without facing the risk of non-payment.

Rental

Instead of buying or committing to a long-term lease, some customers are willing to pay to use (rent) a product for a short period of time. Paradies Shops Inc., one of the nation's largest airport booksellers, is using rentals to attract a new segment of customers—frequent fliers who want to read the latest books but are not willing to pay full price for them. In addition to selling new books, the retailer also rents books. The process works as follows. A customer purchases a new book at its full retail price. Within six months, they can return the book (with proof of purchase) to any of the company's airport locations and receive a 50% refund of what they paid. The store then sells the book as used for 50% of the retail price. This pricing approach serves two types of customers: readers who want to rent a new book and those who want to own a used book at a discounted price.[84] Of course, the books' authors receive royalties only on the first sale, not on any subsequent sales. Contributions to John Grisham can be sent in care of Random House, New York, New York.

Rental pricing is also a cornerstone of the rental-car company Zipcar's business strategy. Targeting auto-less urbanites, the company rents cars by the hour at convenient neighborhood locations. This concept really serves a new market. Since they drive so infrequently and insurance and parking are so expensive, many city-dwellers do not own cars. Zipcar's service offers them the convenience that only a car can provide for running errands and quick excursions. To rent a Zipcar in

Washington, D.C., for example, the hourly rate is between $8.50 and $12.50 (depending on car type). Each rental provides 125 free miles (extra miles are available at eighteen cents per mile), gas, and insurance.

Two-Part Pricing

Two-part pricing, the practice of charging an up-front fixed price as well as additional usage fees, can increase profits and growth by stimulating additional purchases, better capturing value, and serving new customer segments. After paying an up-front fee, customers base their usage on per-use fees. If your idea of a pleasant summer activity is relaxing at a swim club that has an outdoor pool, wouldn't you visit the pool more often (and be happier with the overall experience) if you were charged $200 up-front and $1 for each visit rather than paying no up-front fee and $10 per visit? Costco is one example of a company that uses this technique to encourage purchases and to build customer loyalty. To shop at their superstores, customers have to pay an annual membership fee ranging from $45 to $100. Close to 60% of the chain's profits come from these membership fees, which allows it to price its merchandise only slightly above cost. In fact, Merrill Lynch claims that Costco's prices are usually 15% lower on everything it sells compared to retail stores.[85] These compelling prices create excitement, encourage purchases, and engender loyalty. When their memberships expire, customers reflect on their shopping experiences and decide whether their cumulative savings merit membership renewal. Most customers must think so, as Costco has an impressive 86% renewal rate.[86]

Enterprise Rent-A-Car uses two-part pricing for its weekend car rentals. The car-rental company charges a flat rate of $9.99 per day, as well as an additional twenty-five cents per mile charge for travel above the "free" allotment of a hundred miles per day for an economy car. This $9.99 price is much lower than the $30 daily rates charged by rivals (who offer unlimited mileage). This pricing approach accomplishes two goals. First, this technique allows Enterprise to serve new customers with different valuations. The $30 rate charged by Enterprise's rivals attests to the fact that some customers value the opportunity to not watch the odometer and drive long distances if they so desire. However, a $30 rate is often too high to attract lower-value customers who need a car for more local usage. These customers can be profitable to serve, since they drive so few miles. Enterprise's low base rate enables the company to serve these new customers. Second, Enterprise is better able to capture the value their customers place on renting a car by charging an additional fee for mileage incurred over the 100-mile-per-day allotment.

Hurdles

Hurdles, already discussed as a differential-pricing practice, can also be used to identify new customer segments with different product needs. Time is often used as a means to serve new customers. For example, amusement parks have traditionally offered full-day admission prices. To attract new customers, many parks now offer lower-priced admission after four P.M. This new time-based option attracts locals interested in visiting the park after school or work. Parking garages also use time as a hurdle to serve different customers. It's not unusual for garages in metropolitan areas to charge rates that exceed $10 an hour, with a maximum of $35. This pricing targets customers who are visiting downtown for a few hours. Many of these same garages use pricing specials, such as "In by nine A.M., out by six P.M. for $15" (come in at 9:05? Oh, that will cost you $35 . . .) to attract another segment of customers—workers who commute to downtown. In both of these examples, time is a hurdle to identify, serve, and profit from different customer types.

Payment Plans

As previously discussed, financing can generate profits because the interest that companies charge is greater than their cost of capital. But just as important, the opportunity to spread out payments (as opposed to paying in full up-front) can attract new customers by making the price better fit their monthly budgets. For example, many shoppers cannot absorb the shock of paying $1,648 for a Gateway Widescreen laptop. To increase this product's appeal, the Home Shopping Network (HSN) offers a flex-payment option of making five monthly payments of $329.60. Obviously, in this example, HSN is not charging interest for this monthly payment option. Here the plan is used solely to attract customers who would not otherwise purchase from HSN.

To better serve customers whose expenditures closely match their cash inflows, many car companies offer by-the-week financing, with payments ranging from $49 for a Hyundai Accent to $229 for a Lexus EX300.[87] Similarly, many used-car dealers use the buy-here, pay-here financing method to serve those with poor credit. Interestingly, the requirement that customers visit the dealership to make their weekly payments is a tool used to lower delinquencies. During these visits, salespeople engage in friendly chitchat to try to establish close customer relationships. The hope is that this relationship will make it emotionally difficult to default on payments to a "friend."[88]

Customized Pricing

Customizing pricing can create growth by better tailoring price to how each customer values your product. The prices that result from customized pricing are similar to those divined from individual negotiations. But instead of salespeople using their well-honed instincts to determine price, customized pricing is usually based on a formulaic process that involves inputting customer-specific data. Auto-insurance companies, for example, use hundreds of customer-specific characteristics to create customized price quotes. This allows them to better align prices with a driver's risk profile. This has two benefits. First, insurance companies don't lose money on risky drivers by setting rates that are too low. Second, they can steal customers from rivals who are not using customized pricing. The elderly customer who drives only to make weekly trips to church and the grocery store can be profitably charged lower rates.

Customized pricing has also allowed insurance companies to serve a new set of customers known as "nonstandard" drivers. These drivers range from teenagers driving fast sports cars to drivers who relocated to a state where their established insurance carrier did not offer coverage. Steve Groot, the president of Allstate Indemnity Co. (a unit of Allstate Corp.) echoes a basic theme of this book, saying, "We spent fifty years telling agents that it [insuring nonstandard drivers] was bad business. We found out that at the right price, it was a good business."[89] Customized pricing has generated growth by serving these new customers, as well as selling them additional products like homeowner's and life insurance.

All-You-Can-Eat Pricing

Many of us value the idea of paying one price for the unlimited use of a product. Admittedly, one risk of this approach is that it can attract profit-draining gluttons enamored with the word *unlimited*. But this pricing concept also draws in profitable customers who value its convenience and the peace of mind of not having to make a financial decision about every purchase. For instance, a *New York Times* writer nicely summed up her decision to pay an extra $179 for unlimited alcoholic drinks on her one-week Club Med vacation: "It wasn't that we wanted to booze it up, but we certainly didn't want to think about the cost of every drink or ask ourselves, 'Do I really need this expresso?' "[90] Vacationers have embraced this all-you-can-eat pricing concept. Demand is so strong that more than 50% of all hotel rooms in Jamaica are now at all-inclusive resorts.[91] In addition, for some locations like the Bahamas, up to 80% of all U.K. bookings are made at all-inclusive resorts.[92]

Of course, your price also needs to account for the downside associated with an all-you-can-eat approach—those who literally consume the profits. Red Lobster discovered the hard way that setting the right price is not always easy. In summer 2003, the restaurant chain offered an Endless Crab promotion. For $20 (in some markets, later raised to $25), customers could dine on as many Alaskan Snow Crab legs as they pleased. The pricing tactic was a financial disaster. Joe Lee, the chairman of Darden Restaurants (Red Lobster's parent company) described the perils of an all-you-can-eat approach: "It wasn't the second helping; it was the third one that hurt." Dick Rivera, Darden's COO, added, "Yeah, and maybe the fourth."[93] Some Endless Crab customers literally ate until it hurt (both them and the restaurant chain). This promotion reportedly increased food costs by $31 million and is credited with triggering one of Darden's worst stock routs ever—$405.9 million of its market cap was lost on one September 2003 trading day.[94]

For me, the prices at all-inclusive resorts seem high (a reaction on my part that at this point should not surprise anyone reading this book). I used to regularly stay at the Royal Bahamian Hotel in Nassau, Bahamas. While the hotel had lost some luster since its heyday, when "the Beatles once stayed here," I didn't mind. I loved it. Of course, part of the attraction for me was its price. During the off-season, the hotel offered a "summer special" of buy three nights for $95 per night, get the fourth night free (and they even generously tossed in a $15 bar credit). What a great deal! After not visiting the Bahamas for a few years, I called the hotel to book a reservation. The pleasant reservationist informed me that the hotel had changed ownership and become an all-inclusive resort. Getting into the island spirit, I replied, "No problem" (omitting the customary "mon" ending). She then explained that the price included everything from rooms and meals to all water-sports activities. Again I replied, "No problem." Checking the rates for my dates, she quoted me a price that was more than $500 a night! Now *that* was a problem!

CHAPTER 9

Applying the Finishing Touches

The Art of Pricing

Irving Azoff is known for many things; he is a well-respected personal manager in the music industry, a movie producer, and a record-label chief. But in my book (literally speaking), one of his biggest accomplishments was pioneering pricing for profits and growth in the concert industry for his client the rock group the Eagles. So I was happy for the opportunity to interview him and to better understand his perspective on pricing. What I discovered is that his experience reveals a valuable pricing lesson that is relevant to any product or service: a value-based price is not complete until the finishing touches are applied.

Many people, including myself, consider the Eagles to be one of the greatest bands in rock and roll. They are members of the Rock and Roll Hall of Fame, and *Their Greatest Hits*

1971–1975 has been certified by the Recording Industry Association of America as the best-selling album of *all time*. The band has sold more than 120 million albums worldwide, had five number-one albums, and won four Grammy awards. Irving Azoff has guided the Eagles throughout their career and helped them capitalize on their creative successes.

For better or for worse, the Eagles' 1994 reunion tour is often credited with breaking the concert-ticket-price glass ceiling. Up to that point, the rock-concert industry had been hesitant to set high ticket prices. Bands and their managers did not want to risk upsetting their fans, and they thought low prices would create "friend of the fan" goodwill (there's that word again). As a result, ticket prices were set low, concerts sold out in minutes, and economists indoctrinated by the law of demand and supply screamed: "Raise prices!" Because this was the first time in fourteen years that the Eagles had toured, fans were excited to see the concert. What distinguished this tour, from a pricing perspective, was Irving Azoff's decision to set ticket prices that reached $115 at some venues. Though some entertainment acts had previously set high prices (notably, Barbra Streisand charged $350 for her New York concerts), the Eagles were the first major rock band to set their ticket prices above the critical $100 threshold.

These high prices didn't go unnoticed by the public or by its self-appointed watchdogs. Boston rock station WBCN, for example, staged an "Eagles Greed Weekend." This promotion offered $50 rebates to listeners who couldn't afford Eagles tickets or who just felt that they were too expensive.[95] But instead of causing harm, this radio-station publicity stunt only fueled interest in seeing the band. The Eagles sold out all five of their Boston shows. In fact, the band's abbreviated 1994 tour (shortened due to a group member's illness) ranked number three in concert-revenue grosses,[96] and they were the top-grossing band in 1995.[97] The high ticket prices did not affect the band's music sales, either. The Eagles' *Hell Freezes Over* CD reached the number-one position on the *Billboard* album chart.[98]

Since the high prices did not materially affect concert attendance, the Eagles' story seems to be another exemplary case of using value pricing to uncover hidden profits. Wouldn't you agree? The problem, however, is that Irving refused to agree with this pricing diagnosis in our interview. When I tried to pigeonhole his strategy as value-based pricing, he resisted. Sensing my confusion, Irving finally opened up and shared the secret of his pricing strategy. "Rafi," he said, "we used price to make a statement to fans that they are seeing the greatest American rock-and-roll band, not a washed-up reunion band."[99] What a fascinating use of price! His explanation highlights an important lesson to keep in mind: while the primary role of pricing is to capture value, it has additional capabilities that can help your business profit and grow.

Irving's experience illustrates the last step of pricing—applying the finishing touches. He expanded the scope of pricing beyond just capturing value; indeed, he used price to set a *belief of value* in customers' minds. This capitalized on a reflex that many of us can relate to: a high price usually grabs our attention and, in the process, creates high expectations. While anyone can set a high price, they then have to deliver on the implied promise. With a three-hour-long hit-filled concert that received excellent reviews, the Eagles more than delivered on their pledge of being the greatest American rock-and-roll band.

Up to this point, this book has discussed pricing in terms of value and lessons from an auction. These are the fundamental concepts of pricing. But to quote one of my favorite infomercial marketers, Ron Popeil (seller of such products as the Showtime Rotisserie & BBQ, Dial-O-Matic Food Slicer, and Inside the Shell Egg Scrambler), "But wait—there's more!" The final step involves refining your prices based on the goals of your business and knowledge of your customers.

In this chapter I'm going to show you how to apply the finishing touches to your multi-price mindset pricing strategy. These refinements fall into two categories. First, remember in Chapter 3 when I mentioned that there are times when it makes sense to restrain your prices? Now I'm going to show you the select occasions when, for strategic and fairness reasons, you should consider setting a price that is lower than what a Value Decoder analysis might suggest. Second, while it sounds like a truism, people are only human and there are a host of observed quirks, which I call "purchasing reflexes," in the ways consumers perceive prices. Better understanding these purchasing reflexes may help you formulate your strategies. (For example, while the actual difference is trivial, it's well known that many customers perceive $99.99 to be much lower than $100.)

Strategic Reasons to Rein In Prices

Before setting the price you've derived from your Value De-coder analysis, let me share with you four strategic reasons why you may want to lower that price. Low prices can be used to create publicity, make sure the right customers buy your prod-uct, promote repeat business, and fit the way that customers use price to judge a product.

Low prices can create invaluable marketing publicity. That's exactly what they did for the Broadway version of *The Producers*. Showered with awards and rave reviews, the show has enjoyed a long and profitable run since its April 2001 opening. Even after the show broke (for the first time) the $100 ticket-price barrier for orchestra seats, theatergoers clamored for tickets. The show garnered priceless media cov-erage on the overwhelming demand and ticket-buying antics of consumers. This publicity broke *The Producers* out of the clutter of Broadway theater offerings. The tremendous de-mand also comforted consumers. Combined with the play's fantastic reviews, this strong demand was a sign of approval from fellow theatergoers. Sure, *The Producers* could have charged higher ticket prices, but their forgone profits created invaluable marketing benefits—the hysteria associated with trying to get a ticket served as a constant reminder to theater-goers that *The Producers* is a must-see play. As a result, the play has had an increased Broadway run and successful worldwide touring versions, has enjoyed enhanced merchandise sales, and is being developed as a movie (a remake of the movie the play was based on).

Low prices can also ensure that the right customers get your product. For example, the ticket-buying mania associated with sold-out sporting events again leads economists to chant their market-based chorus: "Raise prices!" What my economics brethren don't understand is that price affects a product's composition of customers. Making sure that the right mix of customers purchase a product has long-term profit implications. For example, as many of you know, the Red Sox baseball team has loyal fans who follow the team regardless of whether they are in first or last place. But when the Red Sox are doing well, a new type of fan emerges: those who are interested for social reasons. During these good times, it becomes fashionable to head to Fenway Park to watch a game.

A stadium filled with wealthy socialites may be profitable in the short run, but if sales to these customers result in loyal fans having to watch the game from home instead of cheering in the stands, this has long-term profit implications. Loyal fans are the lifeblood of any sports team. They closely follow the team, buy merchandise (shirts, hats, etc.), fuel enthusiasm for the game by calling sports talk-radio shows, and watch the games on television. One drawback of these fans (from a pricing perspective) is that they tend to be younger, have lower levels of disposable income, and have already spent a significant chunk of money supporting the team throughout the season. High prices for championship games can result in these valuable customers sitting in cheaper nosebleed seats or, even worse, being ticketless. Teams set low prices (relative to what they could charge) to make sure that these fervent fans get tickets. The hope is that the hurdle of waiting in line for tickets is a reliable loyalty screener. Sure, some tickets find their way to scalpers and are resold at astronomical prices. But that is not necessarily indicative of a pricing-strategy failure. Setting low prices is a success if most tickets end up in the hands of the right customers.

Low prices can promote repeat business as well. We all live by the credo that repeat customers are the key to success. The role that price plays in generating repeat business depends on how frequently a customer can use a product. For instance, my accountant lowering his tax preparation price isn't going to persuade me to do my taxes more than once a year. However, a discounted price *will* get me to wash my car more often. If a lower price can be used to trigger more frequent purchases of your product, don't lose sight of the big picture. In these cases, setting prices becomes more than capturing all the value delivered on one occasion—it's about maximizing profits over time from repeat business.

Low prices can also be used to fit the perceptions customers associate with certain price levels. I am often asked how I used my own advice when it came to pricing this book. I presented a Value Decoder analysis to John, my editor, recommending a $30 price. As I have become accustomed to in our conversations, the tone of his voice made it clear that he disagreed with me (and we all can see whose wisdom prevailed). John's reasoning is interesting; he shared with me that in the book industry, a $30 price point will lead both retailers and customers to believe that a book is too technical and specialized. Our exchange illustrates an important point: in many industries, retailers and customers have ingrained perceptions of different prices. In these instances, it may be wise to set aside your Value Decoder analysis and cede to psychological convention.

In some industries, crossing critical psychological price thresholds can cause explosive growth. This is what happened in 1997 when prices in the personal-computer industry fell below the crucial $1,000 threshold. As one industry observer commented: "This [$1,000] is a magic price. It is the magic price point because it opens [the computer industry] up to this new segment of customers."[100] In addition to drawing in new customers, the computer manufacturer Compaq found that the $1,000 price barrier struck a chord with an unexpected new segment of customers—those who already owned computers. A company spokesman explained the reasoning for these sales: "With prices under a thousand dollars, people and families could easily justify getting a second PC in the home."[101]

Fairness in Pricing

Throughout this book, I've encouraged you to stand up and charge prices that reflect your value. I've tried to suggest that you have to make peace with the idea that you *can* be a nice person and *still* charge the prices that you rightfully deserve. That said, there are occasions when, for fairness reasons, you should exercise some pricing restraint, or even lower prices.

But first, let's be "fair." Sometimes a discount that seems like a generous or fair gesture is actually a competitive necessity. If the "nice" owner of the store next door gives discounts to the local school and the elderly, guess what? Whether you like it or not, you're also going have to be nice to remain competitive. It's business. Casinos in Las Vegas shower loyal customers— from those playing twenty-five-cent slot machines to "whales" betting $1,000 per hand of blackjack—with complimentary gifts (meals, hotel rooms, passes to the Liberace Museum). While these freebies seem generous, I can assure you that they'd be curtailed if rivals exercised restraint in their give-aways. Freebies and low prices enhance rivals' overall values.

That said, let me outline four situations in which fairness is a compelling reason to roll back prices. In these circumstances, it's best to keep your prices in line with common reference prices, by which I mean prices that customers recall or under-stand based on the context in which they are offered (e.g., the reference price of a martini is adjusted if it is served at a fancy club as opposed to a local dive bar). The four situations where fairness is relevant to your pricing strategy are those in which customer types, relationships, transparency, and essential prod-ucts with few substitutes are important. And in each case, some understanding of psychology will go a long way.

1. Customer Types

Who purchases your product? The role that fairness plays in pricing is often related to the types of customers you have. For example, how pricing literate are they? Wall Street executives, who understand the connection between price and value from their daily experiences with the stock market, probably more readily accept the high "captive-audience" value-based refreshment prices at movie cinemas than do other customers who are less attuned to what I've been covering in this book. Try to put yourself in your customers' shoes: while you may be able to justify your price, if your customers are not willing (or able) to accept the explanation, you'll have to back down.

Customers' willingness to understand value heavily influences pricing in the entertainment industry. Movie-studio executives universally recoil when I suggest raising ticket prices for popular films. Their reluctance to raise prices is understandable. Tacking on an extra dollar of profit to a ticket price can transform the infectious enthusiasm young customers often have for an upcoming blockbuster film into angry feelings of, "Hey, The Man is trying to rip us off." In contrast, companies offering entertainment products targeted toward older audiences (who are more at ease with value pricing) are less constrained in setting prices. Few customers complain that the norm to see a Broadway play is now $100, or that the top tickets for the Rolling Stones' 2005 concert tour were priced at more than $450. Pricing in the entertainment industry illustrates an important general rule: be conscious of how willing your customers are to accept a high price.

2. Relationships

Economists spend a lot of time trying to explain the exchange between buyers and sellers. In many cases, a commonsense comparison will do the trick. Often, pricing becomes the basis of a relationship with your customers (especially among your most loyal). And with any relationship, you should be aware of the emotional and psychological dimensions. Think about your favorite store. Initially, your purchasing decisions were made by calculating whether the products provided the best value for your dollar. You purchased products that met this criterion and passed on those that didn't. The relationship was simple back then. But as customers become regulars, most develop a personal relationship with a firm.[102] This can be a friendship with the cheerful proprietor or an affinity for the brand. For example, while I've never personally met anyone with the corporation, I often find myself thinking, "I love Costco." When the relationship reaches this stage, feelings about price usually shift from a laissez-faire "It's business" to the more emotional "It's personal." As we all know from our own personal lives, emotional relationships are a delicate balancing act that, once upset, can shift from "love" to "hate" quickly and irreversibly. If loyal customers feel mistreated by a price, the resulting feelings can be as strong as the pain of a friend's betrayal. This can destroy a profitable bond of trust. In these situations, selectively maintaining low prices and easing long-term customers into higher prices can preserve relationships.

Even so, you shouldn't feel yourself always constrained

from raising prices. Understanding the psychological elements of the pricing relationship you have with loyal customers can provide ways to increase prices and also keep these relationships intact. Customers tend to be amenable, for instance, to increases that are justified by higher costs.[103] Delivery companies like Federal Express used this justification to raise prices. They went to great lengths to explain that because of higher oil costs (which everyone can relate to, from their own experiences at the gas pump), they have to add a fuel surcharge to their delivery prices. Similarly, the customer wrath caused by high prices can be muted by donating a portion of the profit to charities. For instance, returning to the Broadway play *The Producers*, in October 2001 the box office started selling fifty of the choicest orchestra and mezzanine seats at each show for $480. Following the script of fairness, the box office pledged to donate $150 of every $480 ticket sold to the 9/11 Twin Towers Fund for several months.[104]

3. Transparency

I've advocated differential pricing as a cornerstone strategy of the multi-price mindset. Sometimes, if the different prices become too apparent, this strategy can anger customers. For example, I was recently in a department store and watched a manager hand a $25 discount coupon to a customer who was feverishly comparing product prices. Out of a sense of pure research, of course, I asked him for a coupon and was surprised when he refused. While I eventually did get the coupon, it was a struggle. In retrospect, I realize that the manager was practicing exactly what I preach when I talk about the virtues of differential pricing. Since I was casually browsing through merchandise, there was no indication that the coupon would be the factor that led me to the cash register. But for my comparison-shopping counterpart, it was more probable that a discount would clinch the sale. Transparent price differences can create a backlash by angering or alienating your most profitable customers—those who are paying full price. If it's difficult to avoid being transparent, it may be best to curtail your differential pricing.

For example, the textbook-publishing industry is currently facing criticism over its blatant differential pricing practices. Most publishers base their textbook prices on the economy of the country in which the books are sold. As a result, the same textbooks are sold at a 50% discount in some countries relative to their U.S. price (in some instances it may be a paperback rather than hardback book, but the content is the same). For instance, *Linear System Theory and Design, Third Edition,* is priced at $110 in the United States but can be purchased for $49.81 (including shipping) in England. These transparent price differentials led the National Association of College Stores to ask publishers to end this practice, which they see as unfair to American students . . . and, not inconsequentially, as hurtful to their own business.[105] As you can guess, enterprising middlemen are now importing low-priced textbooks from abroad and reselling them at prices that undercut local bookstores. So, in addition to upsetting U.S. customers, this pricing has alienated textbook retailers. One Purdue University bookstore owner could not have been pleased when his Federal

Express deliveryman mentioned that he had just dropped off fourteen skids of textbooks (about fifty books per skid) from India to the Purdue Indian Students Association[106] (I can almost hear his plaintive, "Honey, cancel that trip to the Cayman Islands").

4. Essential Products with Few Substitutes

Companies that sell essential products often face pricing dilemmas. If a product is essential (i.e., valuable to daily life), does this mean that a company's profit margins should be constrained? Suppose you own a hardware store. Are you entitled to increase the price of shovels during a blizzard? Some say, "Sure, it's business." Store owners have taken the risk of purchasing the stock and provide a valuable retail service. Is it fair to the store owner to keep prices low and have his limited supply sell out on a first come, first served basis? Others view such a price increase as taking unfair advantage of customers during a dire situation. What do you think? Would it be okay to increase prices by 20%, instead of 100%? Should you charge a different price to someone you know is going to shovel driveways for profit? Let's totally take the role of relationships out of the equation—suppose you happen to have twenty-five shovels in your attic and decide to resell them on a busy street corner. Now, what price will you set? What if instead of snow shovels during a blizzard, the product is gasoline on a busy highway when people are fleeing an area that is about to be hit by a hurricane? Does this change the way you think about setting prices for an in-demand product? Some people are consumed with solving weighty social problems . . . these are the types of issues that keep *me* up at night.

In these situations, it's important to consider both the legal and psychological consequences of raising prices. Of course, in some situations there are laws against unfair pricing in shortage situations. But what I find more interesting are the moral dilemmas and potential long-term damage to one's reputation that are associated with pricing decisions. Do you have a moral contract with your customers? If shovels are in short supply, is it the right thing to do to sell all of your supply at low prices to customers who line up at seven A.M. and say, "Sorry, we're sold out," to those who arrive after eight A.M.? In addition, often the condition that leads to the shortage—in this case, the snowstorm—is of limited duration, and customers, like elephants, have long memories. Sometimes it's best to forgo these quick profits and live to price another day.

Customers can become outraged when they feel that companies are using pricing power to take advantage of them. Some attribute the riots that occurred at the three-day 1999 Woodstock festival to the pent-up anger fans felt about being gouged for essential refreshments. With drinks priced at $4, hot dogs at $6, and twelve-inch pizzas at $12, one concert attendee opined, "It wasn't Woodstock, it was Commercialstock."[107]

Truly embracing a multi-price mindset may in some cases provide a way to avoid the horns of this dilemma. Take lifesaving drugs as a case in point. Most pharmaceutical companies have pricing programs that offer discounted prices to patients without drug coverage. For example, ten drug-makers have launched a Together Rx Access discount card aimed at the

36 million working-age, low-income Americans who lack health insurance. Offering discounts ranging from 25% to 40%, this card is available to legal U.S. residents younger than sixty-five with annual incomes under $30,000, or $60,000 for a family of four.[108] While these programs benefit society, they are also part of these companies' multi-price mindset pricing strategies (a differential pricing tactic of using hurdles to identify customers who are not willing or able to pay full price).

Price As a Marketing Tool

At long last, we've reached the final step of pricing—making your pricing strategy not only work, but sparkle. This section discusses psychological tools that can make your price even more appealing to customers. These time-tested strategies (that we can all relate to) have little to do with equating price with value. Instead, they tap into the subjective ways that we process and act on the prices we encounter. So, as you are polishing your price, keep the following eight strategies in mind:

1. The Nine and Zero Effect

A common finishing touch is to end a price with a nine to make it appear lower ($7.99 seems lower than $8). Researchers have advanced this theory by finding that customers associate prices that end with a nine with value and those that finish with a zero with quality. This interesting revelation is often illustrated in pricing practices within a product line. Firms offering lower-end products tend to end their prices with nines, while those offering higher-end products wrap up their prices with zeros.[109] Think about your own dining experiences. Most fast-food chains end their prices with nines, while prices at star chefs' restaurants usually end with zeros.

2. Payments to Promote Satisfaction

Product satisfaction is generally correlated with usage. Customers who use a product frequently tend to gain higher satisfaction relative to those who don't. What's interesting, from a psychological standpoint, is that the structure of a pricing plan can affect usage. Researchers recently studied the payment and attendance records of members at a prestigious health club. These members were contractually committed to $600 one-year memberships. The club allowed payments to be made annually, semi-annually, quarterly, or monthly. The researchers found that as time passed after a payment, customers started viewing their memberships as "free" and worked out less. For those who chose the one-annual-payment option, their workout frequency in the final months of membership was only a quarter of what it had been in the first few months. The same pattern prevailed for those on semi-annual and quarterly plans: a cycle of heightened workouts after payment that slowly deteriorated until the next payment. Attendance for members on the monthly plan was the most constant.[110] The implication of this research is that payment structure can promote satisfaction by stimulating usage.

3. Prestige Pricing

Consumers often associate high prices with prestige. Absolut Vodka leveraged this price-prestige association and pioneered today's booming super-premium liquor market. Upon its introduction in 1979, the Swedish vodka company charged the unheard-of price of $13 a bottle for a spirit that many consider to be odorless, tasteless, and colorless. This premium-pricing approach made marketing history. The price grabbed consumers' attention; instead of ordering a vodka tonic, it became a sign of good taste to order an Absolut and tonic. Within five years of its introduction, Absolut was (and remains) the best-selling imported vodka in the United States.

4. Anchor Pricing

For products they are unfamiliar with, customers tend to use the highest-priced model within a category as an anchor on which to base their decisions. Starting with the top price, customers evaluate whether the trade-off of fewer attributes of rival products are worth the lower price. For example, in the private-label-product industry, the rule of thumb is that to account for not having a well-known reputation, the price should be at least 15% lower than that of the branded product.[111] One implication of anchoring is that you should not set a price that is too low relative to those of established products. Commenting on this phenomenon, one private-label industry consultant makes a claim that resonates with many of us: "Once you get outside the customer's comfort zone, the consumer psychology becomes 'Gee, they must have taken out the quality.' " [112]

5. Quantity-Suggestive Pricing

Shoppers are often receptive to purchasing the quantity of products that is suggested in a pricing structure. I suspect that we've all succumbed to purchasing larger quantities when a sale on Ramen Noodles is phrased as ten packages for $1 instead of ten cents apiece. Researchers have tested how the phrasing of a price affects sales. In their experiment, some stores just set a lower price (e.g., two-liter soft drinks priced at $1.49 each—a 17% discount) while other stores phrased the sale in terms of quantity (e.g., two bottles of soda for $3.00). The products in the study, which ranged from bathroom tissue to tuna, were discounted on average by 21%. Researchers found that when prices were simply discounted, average sales rose by 125%. However, when prices were phrased in terms of quantity, sales rose by 165%.[113]

6. Large Versus Small Losses

In addition to providing financing that fits consumers' monthly budgets, phrasing prices in smaller increments can make a price more appealing. Ron Popeil, the infomercial king, tends to pose his prices in terms of payment installments. For instance, the price of his Showtime Professional Rotisserie &

BBQ is prominently billed as "eight easy payments of $31.95." Mention of the one single payment price option of $255.60 is almost an afterthought. Consumers tend to perceive a series of small losses as less than one large loss, even when the series equals the one large loss. Eight payments of $31.95 or one payment of $255.60—what sounds more appealing to you?

7. Stuffing the Bundle to Convey Value

Firms often stuff bundles with a variety of tangential extras to convey the impression of value. Many of us are familiar with the fast-talking television pitches for the Ginsu knife. It's hard not to come away from these commercials thinking that $19.99 for a set of knives that carry a lifetime warranty and the promise of never needing sharpening is a great deal. The value is further sweetened by the presentation of the $19.99 price as a bundle that includes eight steak knives, a spreader, a fruit and vegetable knife, a utility knife, a carving/slicing knife, a bread knife, a chef's knife, a spiral slicer, a food decorator, shears, and a garnish/decoration cookbook. While I doubt that I'll ever use the garnish/decoration cookbook, you have to admit that the idea of getting a twenty-two-piece knife set for $19.99 seems remarkable.

8. Everyone Loves a Bargain

Let's face it, many of us enjoy the hunt and thrill of purchasing products that are highly discounted. Banners announcing 30%

to 50% discounts aren't always about adjusting a price to value; they can be used to attract "Looking for Mr. Good Deals" customers who pride themselves on not paying retail prices.[114] Reflecting this interest in good deals, a senior vice president for ACNielsen recently commented, "Poor people need low prices [value]. Wealthy people love low prices [psychology]."[115] High percentage discounts tap into customers' desire to feel that they got a good deal.

The Final Touches to Price

For most products, the vast majority of work involved in bringing the product to market involves heavy-lifting tasks such as design and production. Yet it is the relatively small finishing touches, like color and packaging, that heavily influence purchasing decisions. The same is true for pricing. The heavy lifting of pricing involves better understanding how customers value your product and designing strategies to capitalize on lessons from an auction. But almost as important are the easy-to-implement psychological tactics discussed in this chapter, which can be the difference between a good and a great pricing strategy.

CHAPTER **10**

It All Starts on Monday Morning

Memo to the Manager: Pricing for Profits and Growth

Congratulations on being a manager! To make it this far, you've distinguished yourself through your selling abilities, outstanding work, or being a trusted go-to person who always gets the job done. Being promoted to manager acknowledges your intelligence, hard work, conscientiousness, and the personal sacrifices you've made. But along with this recognition comes a new duty: the responsibility of consistently growing your division's profits every year. This is a tricky transition point in your career because prior to being promoted to manager, you probably didn't have a lot of experience in growing a division's profits. Now it's the primary metric of your success. Being able to claim, "I increased my division's profits by fifteen percent" is equivalent to hitting a grand-slam

204

home run—you're golden. Growing profits will lead to your next promotion, move to another company, job security, or a confident smile amid the friendly competition with other managers.

Since you're on the hook to constantly deliver more profits, it's hard not to have moments of anxiety and wonder, "How am I going to top last year?" Many choose to take on expensive and risky ventures that may or may not bear profits at a later date. I think the quickest and easiest route to growing profits is to adopt a pricing for profits and growth philosophy. For most companies, pricing is an underutilized strategy that holds the potential to generate big new profits. Best of all, many of my pricing for profits and growth ideas can start working for you on Monday morning. The reason new profits can be uncovered so quickly is that they currently exist in your product. Since most companies think about (and implement) pricing in the wrong manner, their products are loaded with hidden profits. Pricing for profits and growth is a low-risk/high-upside concept that enables you to collect the hidden profits that are rightfully yours and, in the process, keep your star shining brightly.

The Culture of Profit

The first step to uncovering your hidden profits is to give your division a profit tune-up to create a culture of profit. A few straightforward initiatives can have powerful effects on your bottom line. Your first step should be to explain to everyone in your division the value that your product offers consumers.

While this seems obvious, few companies make it a priority. This simple step reaps two benefits. First, your employees will be able to better articulate your product's value and confidently justify its price. Second, this knowledge enables employees to recommend the products that best fit your customers' needs. And if their suggestions happen to be for one of your more expensive (i.e., higher-margined) products, all the better.

To create a culture of profit, you have to realize that pricing is a company-wide issue. Many of your employees touch prices and, as a result, exert some control over your bottom line. For example, your sales force and supervisors are usually empowered to change prices. Marketing and finance departments offer promotions that effectively lower your product's net price. Everyone needs to realize that seemingly minor price tweaks can create large swings in your profits. To make this point clear, I suggest sharing with your employees data on your operating margins. Most will be surprised to see how lean your profit margins are and in the process will realize that their work directly impacts your bottom line. In Chapter 2 I mentioned a study that found that a 1% net price increase will, on average, boost operating profits by 11%. A 1% change in price is a small amount. My bet is that once your employees understand that their actions can make the difference between a good year and a great one, they'll be proactive in trying to achieve the 1% price increase. As you're contemplating how to meet next year's profit goals, a relatively easy 11% increase in operating profits (from raising the price by 1%) is nice to have in your back pocket!

Sharing your operating profit margins is a step in the right direction, but your sales force needs more. They should know the profit margins on each of your products. Of course, I understand your reluctance to share this data. It's always risky to circulate this type of proprietary information. It may be leaked, or someone in your organization may defect to a rival company. If this happens, your competitors will know more about your company than they should. But consider the downside of not sharing this information. Your sales force is a critical link to your customers. Since these employees have the ability to influence what customers purchase, shouldn't they concentrate on selling your highest-margin products? The only way that your sales force can make you the most money is knowing which high-profit products they should be pushing.

The final step to creating a culture of profit involves reviewing your division's pricing policies, marketing promotions, and metrics of success used to evaluate employee performance. Much like in life, it's enlightening to occasionally step back to understand what's working and what needs to be changed. How can you improve your pricing policies? Are the right customers getting the right prices? Do your promotions have profit-leaking "holes" that savvy customers are taking advantage of? Are you evaluating and compensating your staff in a manner that maximizes your division's profits? Sometimes policies get set over the years and just remain due to inertia. Strategically pruning these policies can be a catalyst to growth.

Here's an example of why everyone needs to understand how their actions affect your bottom line. I recently purchased a camera ($350) and an extra digital memory card ($100) on the Internet from a major retailer. One benefit of purchasing from this retailer's website is that I can return merchandise to any of the company's local stores. I decided to return the memory card at my local store and was surprised when the store refunded me the sales tax on the full amount of my purchase ($22.50) instead of just on the product I returned ($5). When I mentioned the excessive refund ($17.50), the clerk mumbled, "We always have this problem with Internet sales, so I just go by what the computer says." When I pushed the issue (I like this store and want it to succeed), he shrugged and continued processing the refund. I later reviewed the company's annual report and discovered that its net profits are 1.7% of total revenues. This means that on average, it makes $5.95 of net profit from the camera I purchased. Because of the computer glitch, the retailer will now have to sell three more cameras to make up for the net profits lost from erroneously refunding me the extra $17.50 in sales tax. Obviously, mistakes happen. The real problem was the clerk's attitude. I doubt that he'll make an effort to ensure that this problem doesn't occur again. This type of ambivalence is exactly why you need to establish a culture of profit in your division: you want everyone to be proactively looking for and plugging these types of profit leaks.

The Foundation of Pricing: Value

One of your highest priorities should be to instill the right way to think about pricing into your organization; prices need to be aligned with the value customers place on your product. Most companies have yet to adopt this fundamental pricing principle. Instead, they base their prices on how they've always done it, seat-of-the-pants analysis, or—most commonly—just marking up their costs. Think about your own purchases. You formulate the amount that you are willing to pay based on how you value a product, not on what it costs the manufacturer to make it. So if customers use value to determine the amount they are willing to pay, why should your company base its prices on costs? Seeing price as a reflection of value is essential to uncovering your product's hidden profits. Remember the street vendors in Chapter 3 who raised their umbrella prices at the first hint of rain? Their savvy actions illustrate the pricing mantra that your division needs to adopt: "It's all about value." A company that is focused on value promotes growth, in addition to capturing higher profits. Everyone should be on the lookout for new opportunities to enhance your product in ways that customers will value and be willing to pay premiums for.

The link between value and price is easy to understand because we experience it in our everyday lives. We regularly make decisions about whether a product is worth more (in terms of value) than its price. To determine your product's value, you need to understand what's going on in the minds of consumers when they make these snap purchasing judgments. I reveal this process in Chapter 5, with my Value Decoder framework that helps guide you in setting your product's price.

The Multi-Price Mindset

Understanding the role of value in pricing is a great start to uncovering your hidden profits. However, there are more profits to be captured. Most companies are handicapped by the way they view pricing; they approach it as a search for their product's "one perfect price." These companies, by definition (even if their prices are based on value), have hidden profits. Remember my friend David Straus from Chapter 1? Think about the hidden profits he would have if he thought of pricing as a search for the perfect ($18 or $31) price. To uncover your product's hidden profits, you have to think about pricing in terms of early-bird, regular, and chef's-table strategies.

The real epiphany to pricing for profits and growth comes from understanding a concept that I term "lessons from an auction." Lessons from an auction represent the fact that different customers value your product differently. Some are willing to pay more than others are. This anomaly is what expands pricing beyond just setting the right price into a powerful business strategy that can generate continued growth. The key to pricing for profits and growth is capitalizing on lessons from an auction by adopting a multi-price mindset. Since customers value your product differently, your pricing strategy should aim to make more money from those who are willing to pay high prices (e.g., chef's-table seating), and use discounts to sell to those who have lower valuations (e.g., early-bird specials). This is exactly what a multi-price mindset accomplishes. It encourages managers to view pricing as a series of strategies that allow them to serve the broadest range of customers and reap different profit margins based on the values purchasers place on the product. A multi-price mindset is composed of three core strategies: differential pricing, versioning, and segment-based pricing.

Every company should use differential pricing, the strategy of charging different prices to different customers. Differential pricing allows you to understand the amount each customer is willing to pay and to charge them accordingly. Chapter 6 showed you how to get customers to reveal how much they value your product by using the following tactics: customer characteristics, setting hurdles, charging different prices over time, quantity discounts, base prices on distribution points, mixed bundling, and individual negotiation. As a consumer, you've undoubtedly experienced differential pricing. Chances are that you've been in a grocery-store checkout line when the person ahead of you used a coupon for an item that you were also buying. As a result, you paid more for that product than the coupon-clipper did. Coupons allow companies to target and sell their products to customers with lower valuations. Customers who make the effort to redeem coupons are revealing their lower product valuation.

Versioning is a multi-price mindset strategy that involves offering a series of products—typically good (low margin), better (higher margin), and best (highest margin)—that are based on a core product. The goal of this strategy is to allow customers to choose the item that best fits their valuation. Chapter 7 provided seven methods to version your product, through offering a la carte options, more attributes, less attributes, targeted new features (horizontal versioning), expedited service, options to avoid waiting, and products with different levels of uncertainty (in terms of availability and price). We've all had to decide, for example, between versions when choosing steaks for a summer barbecue. Most butcher shops sell select (good), choice (better), and prime (best) quality grades of beef.

Segment-based pricing is my personal favorite multi-price mindset pricing strategy. This strategy activates dormant customers by offering new pricing options for purchasing your product. It capitalizes on the fact that there may be segments of customers who are interested in your product but simply aren't purchasing because your pricing strategy doesn't fit their needs. New pricing options can activate these consumers. These pricing approaches (discussed in Chapter 8) include interval ownership, mixed bundling, leasing, prepaid, rental, two-part pricing, hurdles, payment plan, customized, and all-you-can-eat options. Segment-based pricing is an integral reason for the success of Apple's iTunes electronic music store. Before the iTunes service, you could legally rent (pay a monthly subscription fee to listen to) but not buy electronic music. Apple uses a different pricing tactic; it allows customers to purchase songs for ninety-nine cents each. In announcing its pricing strategy, Steve Jobs declared, "We think subscriptions are the wrong path. We think people want to own their music."[116] In its first week, iTunes sold more than a million songs (the amount Apple had hoped to sell in its first month). With these sales, it instantly became the largest online music company in the world.[117] This sales statistic is even more impressive when you consider that at the time, iTunes served only customers who used an Apple computer (which constituted less than 1% of home computers in the United States) and its portable iPod music-listening devices.[118]

Aligning your price with value and adopting a multi-price mindset are the fundamentals of pricing for profits and growth. There are, however, a few other issues to keep in mind when developing your pricing strategy. For example, lower-than-normal prices can create valuable marketing publicity, ensure that core customers (who may not be able to afford a higher price) get your product during times of high demand, promote repeat business, and conform to convention (e.g., setting a low price for hardware tools may make professional homebuilders think that the tools are only for weekend amateurs). There are also select times when prices should be kept low for fairness reasons. These occasions include situations when bad publicity could result because customers won't accept a high price, hiking prices could destroy a profitable relationship, customers become irate from seeing others offered lower prices, or products are essential during times of crisis (e.g., bottled water after a natural disaster). In these cases, while a Value Decoder analysis may suggest a higher price, moral and long-term strategic considerations dictate restraint. Finally, there are a variety of psychological strategies that can make your price more appealing. For instance, phrasing your price as eight payments of $31.95 makes it sound like less than one payment of $255.60.

What Hidden Profits Can You Uncover Today?

The best way to start uncovering your hidden profits is to tap into your employees' insights and experiences (especially those of your sales force). They are on the front line every day, interacting with your clients. They know what customers value, who will pay more for your product, and which prospects can be converted into buyers by a discount. Your employees are a treasure trove of pricing information. The challenge is in organizing their insights in a constructive manner that enables you to price for profits and growth. To accomplish this, I suggest inviting your colleagues who are involved with setting prices to a pricing summit to discuss the following topics:

- The value that your product or service offers consumers.

- Profit-margin data and incentives for the sales force to sell your most profitable products. Inquire about what other information is needed to help make more profits for the company.

- What policies (pricing, promotions, metrics to evaluate employee performance, and compensation) are conducive to making your company the most money, and which ones aren't.

- Finding and fixing current profit leaks.

- Does your price reflect how customers value your product? What new attributes will customers value?

- Differential pricing and what types of differential-pricing tactics can be implemented.

- Versioning and ideas on how to apply it to your product.

- Segment-based pricing and ideas on identifying dormant customers, as well as new pricing strategies that can activate your dormant customers.

- Other strategic or fairness issues that should be factored into your price, and psychological tactics (e.g., use quantity-suggestive pricing—two for $5 instead of $2.50 each) that can make your price more appealing to customers.

A Few Last Points

Like me, you may find that the ideas in this book help you make better buying decisions in your everyday life. You now understand the "secrets" to getting the best price, and you also have a structured way to judge whether all the bells and whistles of a top-of-the-line product are worth the premium. Is it really worth taking your beach vacation in late August when you can save 25% by switching to the first week of September? I now save twenty cents a gallon by filling up with regular instead of premium gas. I'm not sure why I bought premium gas in the first place—my best guess is because my father always does (and well, exploring that issue probably belongs in a completely different and far more complex book). I've also switched to a few higher-priced products. For instance, I used to think to myself, "That's crazy" when my colleagues took a $40 car service (as opposed to a $25 taxi) from our offices in Cambridge to Logan Airport. But I now appreciate the value of using a car service even though it costs more—about the only thing you can count on in taking a local taxi is that the SERVICE NEEDED light on the dashboard will be shining brightly. Otherwise, uncertainty rules: they'll show up late, take you on a "special" route (note: in the context of pricing, *special* is rarely a good word), or try to pick up other passengers. And most drivers seem to think that you prefer *not* having the air conditioning on during sweltering summer days. In contrast, the car service is always on time, the cars are always nice, and there's never a hassle. Suddenly that extra $15 seems worth it!

You are at a critical and exciting tipping point in your career. You can distinguish yourself in the business world by establishing a track record of growing profits. Sure, there are going to be tough times. But don't forget that you've made it this far because you impressed your colleagues, and they believe in you. I hope that you share my enthusiasm about pricing for profits and growth. It's a powerful concept that, as Lloyd Hansen demonstrated at Ford, can lead you into that coveted corner office on the executive floor. I also hope that you'll have fun designing your pricing strategy—it's always thrilling to watch new pricing initiatives uncover hidden profits.

Keep in touch and start making plans for that celebratory vacation to the Cayman Islands!

Best wishes,
Rafi

NOTES

1. Interview with Lloyd Hansen, February 4, 2004, Dearborn, Michigan.

2. Sidney Hill, Jr., "Target Customers and the Price Is Right: Manugistics Updates Users on Profit Optimization Solutions," *CFO Magazine*, July, 2000.

3. Peter Coy, "The Power of Smart Pricing," *BusinessWeek*, April 10, 2000, p. 160.

4. Hansen interview.

5. David Magee, *Ford Tough: Bill Ford and the Battle to Rebuild America's Automaker* (New York: John Wiley & Sons, 2004), p. 137.

6. Hansen interview.

7. Brent Schlender, Scott McNealy, and Jack Welch, "The Odd Couple," *Fortune*, May 1, 2000.

8. Cliff Peale, "P&G Trying to Determine When Price Is Right," *Cincinnati Enquirer*, September 30, 2001.

9. Michael V. Marn, Eric V. Roegner, and Craig C. Zwanda, *The Price Advantage* (New York: John Wiley & Sons, 2004), p. 5.

10. Alan B. Krueger, "Music Sales Slump, Concert Costs Jump and Rock Fans Pay the Price," *New York Times*, October 17, 2002, p. C-2.

11. "Venue Change," *Buffalo News*, August 14, 2003, p. C-2.

12. Interview with Ron Tadross, March 25, 2004.

13. Zachery Kouwe, "Pizza Delivery Now Costs More Dough—with Sales Flat, Chains Slap Fees on Service to Your Door; Cranky Counts the Pepperoni," *Wall Street Journal*, August 19, 2003, p. D1.

14. Marn, et al., *The Price Advantage*, p. 5.

15. J. Lynn Lunsford, "Dog Fight—Behind Slide in Boeing Orders: Weak Sales Team or Firm Prices?" *Wall Street Journal*, December 23, 2004, p. A1.

16. Hansen interview.

17. Jane Costello, "Shopper Turns Lots of Pudding into Free Miles," *Wall Street Journal* (interactive edition), January 24, 2000.

18. Jane Costello, "The Pudding Guy Flies Again (and Again) Over Latin America," *Wall Street Journal* (interactive edition), March 16, 2000.

19. Marn, et al., *The Price Advantage*, p. 27.

20. Ibid, pp. 24–37.

21. Interview with Ron Robbins, March 25, 2004.

22. Henry M. Vogel, J. Kevin Bright, and George Stalk, Jr., "Organizing for Pricing," The Boston Consulting Group Perspectives, 2002.

23. For more information on pet rocks, please see: http://www.virtual pet.com/vp/farm/petrock/petrock.htm (accessed March 29, 2005).

24. Alexandra Peers, "It's Going . . . Going . . . Gone! Ripken Memorabilia Soars," *Wall Street Journal*, October 6, 1995, p. B11.

25. Timothy Aeppel, "Survival Strategies: After Cost Cutting, Compa-

nies Turn Towards Price Rises—They Don't Call Them That, but Some Trim Discounts and Add New Prices—Charging Extra for Large Sizes," *Wall Street Journal,* September 18, 2002, p. A1.

26. Peter Fritsch, "Jumbo Brawl: As Shrimp Industry Thrives in Vietnam, Trade Fight Looms," *Wall Street Journal,* October 21, 2004, p. A1.

27. Michelle Higgins, "Getting Skewered by Shrimp Prices—Consumers Pay Top Dollar Despite Growing Global Gut; Weighing in at $46 a Pound," *Wall Street Journal,* October 16, 2003, p. D1.

28. Alex Gove, "Margin of Error—Internet Retailers Ponder a World of Zero Gross Margins," *Red Herring,* February 1, 1999, p. 63.

29. Benjamin A. Holden, "Quake Price-Gouging Is Tempting but Short Sighted—In Addition to Possible Legal Penalties, Customers Will Remember It," *Wall Street Journal,* January 27, 1994, p. B2.

30. Julian F. Barnes, "Sony Toy Is Less Costly," *New York Times,* December 17, 2000, p. 39.

31. Tim Bonfield, "The Doctor Will See You—for $1,500," *Cincinnati Enquirer,* January 22, 2003.

32. Timothy Aeppel, "Survival Strategies."

33. John Innes, "Extended Warranties 'Not Rip Off' Says Retailers," Business.Scotman.com, April 26, 2003, p. 3C.

34. AFX News Limited, "GM Auto Profits Fall, but Finance Unit Helps Out—Update 2," AFX.com, January 20, 2004.

35. Harvey Chipkin, "Saturday Night Fever. (No Longer the Loneliest Night for Hotels)," *Travel Weekly,* February 27, 1992.

36. Sarah Schaefer Munoz, "Dieters Track Down Elusive Laughing Cow Cheese," *Wall Street Journal,* April 1, 2004.

37. "Bidding Frenzy for Potter Clue," CNN.com/Entertainmment, http://edition.cnn.com/2002/SHOWBIZ/News/12/12/auction.potter/ (accessed March 29, 2005).

38. Nick Wingfield, "Amazon Offers to Rent DVDs by Mail in the United Kingdom," *Wall Street Journal*, December 10, 2004, p. A11.

39. Nick Wingfield, "Netflix Profit More than Doubles," *Wall Street Journal*, January 25, 2005, p. B4.

40. Janice Castro, "This Industry Is Always at the Grip of Its Dumbest Competitors," *Time*, May 4, 1994, p. 52.

41. Maury Klein, *The Life and Legend of Jay Gould* (Baltimore: The Johns Hopkins University Press, 1986), pp. 96–97.

42. James T. Areddy, "Leader of the Pack Is Black and White and Sought All Over," *Wall Street Journal*, May 26, 2004, p. A1.

43. Robert J. Serling, *From the Captain to the Colonel* (New York: The Dial Press, 1980), p. 369.

44. Ibid, p. 361.

45. Interview with Lloyd Hansen, May 26, 2004.

46. Dominic O'Connell, "Space Tourism Ready to Take Off," *Sunday Times* (London), October 10, 2004, p. 1 (Business section).

47. Michael Wines, "Loss of the Shuttle: Soyuz," *New York Times*, February 4, 2003, p. A24.

48. "307,000 Bid for a Buffett Lunch," *The New Zealand Herald*, July 12, 2004.

49. Sholnn Freeman, "GM Discounts Hummer as Sales Slide," *Wall Street Journal*, May 7, 2004, p. A3.

50. CBSNEWS.com, "Hummer Mania," February 3, 2003, http://www.cbsnews.com/stories/2003/08/07/national/main567097.shtml (accessed March 29, 2005).

51. Lee Hawkins Jr., "The Hummer Gets Downsized—as Sales of the Giant SUV Drop, GM Plans a Smaller Version That Is More Fuel Efficient," *Wall Street Journal*, October 21, 2004, p. D1.

52. Frank J. Prial, "Wine Talk," *New York Times,* December 25, 1991, p. 29.

53. Peter Kupfer, "Revisiting the French Paradox," *Wine Enthusiast,* February 2003.

54. See http://www.thegag.com/forum-24902.html (accessed March 29, 2005).

55. Steven E. Landsburg, "Taken to the Cleaners: Nobody Can Explain Why Laundries Charge Less for Men's Shirts Than for Women's," *Slate,* July 3, 1998, http://slate.msn.com/default.aspx?id=2050 (accessed March 29, 2005).

56. Laura Bird, "Victoria's Secret May Be That Men Get a Better Deal—Suit Alleges Lingerie Catalog Offered a Bigger Discount to Rich Guy Than Woman," *Wall Street Journal,* January 3, 1996, p. B5.

57. Sally Beatty, "Paying Less for Prada—as Sales Slump, Outlet Malls Draw More High-end Labels; 70% Off a Dior Evening Gown," *Wall Street Journal,* April 29, 2003, p. D1.

58. Sarah Ellison, "European Court Supports Levi Strauss in Tesco Case—Decision Gives Manufacturers Control over Distribution, Pricing of Brands in EU," *Wall Street Journal,* November 21, 2001, p. A11.

59. Ray Marcelo, "Officials See Red over Handset Sales: In India up to 9 out of 10 Mobile Phones Are Supplied by Unauthorized Sources," *Financial Times,* October 3, 2003.

60. W.J. Adams and Janet Yellen, "Commodity Bundling and the Burden of Monopoly," *Quarterly Journal of Economics,* August 1976, pp. 475–498.

61. Yannis Bakos and Erik Brynjolfsson, "Bundling Information Goods:

Pricing, Profits, and Efficiency," *Management Science,* Vol. 45, No. 12, 1999, pp. 1613–1630.

62. Paul Szuchman, "Events: Well Aren't You Special—Clubs, Airlines, and Theaters Lower the Bar for VIP Status; Vegas Important Person, $30," *Wall Street Journal,* May 14, 2004, p. W1.

63. Jeffrey A. Trachtenberg, "Title Role: Barnes & Noble Pushes Books From Ambitious Publisher: Itself—Retailer Will Give Its Imprint of Cut-price Offerings Top Placement in Stores—Growing Clout of Wal-Mart," *Wall Street Journal,* June 18, 2003, p. A1.

64. Jesse Drucker, "Sprint's Role as Wholesaler: 'Arms Dealer' to the Industry," *Wall Street Journal,* May 21, 2004, p. B1.

65. Saul Hansell, "Gates vs. Jobs: the Rematch," *New York Times,* November 14, 2004, p. 1 (Business section).

66. Earle Eldridge, "For $85,000, You Could Ride Like P. Diddy," *USA Today,* June 12, 2003, p. 3B.

67. Michelle Higgins, "Getting Your Own IT Department—Best Buy, CompUSA, Others Now Send Techies to Homes; Getting TiVo Set Up for $150," *Wall Street Journal,* May 20, 2004, p. D1.

68. Charles Fishman, "The Wal-Mart You Don't Know," *Fast Company,* December, 2003, Issue 77, p. 68.

69. Ramin Setooodeh, "Step Right Up!—Amusement-Park Visitors Pay Premium to Avoid Long Lines; Some Have-nots Are Miffed," *Wall Street Journal,* July 12, 2004, p. B1.

70. Stenley W. Angrist, "Wine Before Its Time? (Buying Wine Futures)," *Forbes,* March 11, 1985.

71. "The Wine Club Reports $18 million in Bordeaux Sales for 2001; $11 Million in Sales for 2000 Futures Alone," *Business Wire,* March 1, 2002.

72. Fred Ahrens, "Peddling Prime Time; Advertisers Again Spend the Most on NBC, but CBS Edges Closer," *Washington Post*, June 15, 2004, p. E01.

73. Emily Nelson and Suzanne Vranica, "Demand Is Strong for Time on TV—Networks and Ad Agencies Discuss Prices for the Fall Possibly Increasing by 15%," *Wall Street Journal*, March 10, 2003, p. B4.

74. Andy Pasztor and Anne Marie Squeo, "For Sale: Used Jet, Low Miles, Nice Interior—Prices on Private Planes Take Big Dive as Economy Sputters; Finally, a Flying Foldout Bed," *Wall Street Journal*, September 5, 2002, p. D2.

75. Matt Stearns, "For Yacht and Jet Salesmen to the Wealthy, Times Are Good," *Kansas City Star*, March 30, 2004.

76. Anne Marie Squeo, "Downturn Finds Private Jets Flying High—Planes Emerge as Necessity for Time-strapped Executives," *Wall Street Journal*, April 23, 2001, p. A2.

77. Ian Goold, "Fractionals Dominate Airframers' Order Books," *Aviation International News Online*, February 2003.

78. Susan Carey, "Ultimate Upgrade: More Fliers Decide that 1st Class Just Isn't Good Enough—in Blow to Big Carriers, NetJets Sells Shares in Tiny Planes to Expanding Rich Niche—'No Way to Justify Cost,' " *Wall Street Journal*, April 23, 2002, p. A1.

79. Shawn Young, "Technology (A Special Report): Telecommunications—All in One: Buying Bundles of Telecom Services Can Make Things Easier—and Cheaper—for Consumers; the Trick Is Picking the Right Bundle," *Wall Street Journal*, September 13, 2004, p. R6.

80. Eric Schlosser, *Fast Food Nation: The Dark Side of the All-American Meal* (New York: Houghton Mifflin Company, 2001), p. 47.

81. Rod Taylor, "The Beanie Factor," *Brandweek,* June 16, 1997.

82. Steve Finlay, "The Rise and Fall of Automotive Leasing," *Ward's Dealer Business,* March 1, 2004, p. 3.

83. Ruth Simon, "A New Alternative to Monthly Minutes—Cellphone Companies Push Prepaid Calling Cards, but Are They Really a Better Deal?" *Wall Street Journal,* June 4, 2002, p. D1.

84. Jeffrey A. Trachtenberg, "Selling Back 'The Da Vinci Code'—to Lure Frequent Fliers, Airport Bookseller Offers to Repurchase Used Copies,' " *Wall Street Journal,* November 24, 2004, p. D1.

85. Margaret Web Pressler, "Spreeing is Believing: On a First Trip to a Discount Phenomenon, Resistance Wavers," *Washington Post,* June 6, 2004, p. F5.

86. Ibid, p. F5.

87. Stuart Innes, "Time to Pay," *Adelaide Advertiser,* August 17, 2002.

88. Arlena Sawyers, "Silver Lining: Dealers Can Cash In on Subprime Business if They're Willing to Take the Risk," *Automotive News,* November 24, 2003, Volume 78, Publication number 6068.

89. Anne Colden, "Car Insurers Are Courting Risky Drivers—Profits Can Be High on 'Nonstandard' Operators," *Wall Street Journal,* November 10, 1997.

90. Crystal Catto, "Winter in the Sun; by Crystal Seas, Club Med, 2 Ways," *New York Times,* October 20, 2002, p. 8 (section 5).

91. Thomas Sylburn, Jamaica & Dep. HRI Food Service Sector GAIN Report. USDA Foreign Agricultural Service, 2003, p. 6.

92. For more information, please see: http://www.researchandmarkets.com/reportinfo.asp?report_id=3483&cat_id=91 (accessed March 29, 2005).

93. Benita D. Newton, "All-You-Can-Eat Was Too Much," *St. Petersburg Times,* September 26, 2003, p. 1A.

94. Paul Tharp, "Red Lobster Promos: A Claws for Concern," *New York Post*, March 20, 2004, p. 19.

95. Dean Johnson, "Boston Radio Band and WBCN Trade Blows Over 'Eagles Greed,' " *Boston Herald*, August 9, 1994, p. 45.

96. Richard Harrington, "The Road Warriors: '94 Concert Tours Set Record," *Washington Post*, January 4, 1995, p. B7.

97. Richard Harrington, "Eagles Take it to the Limit in '95," *Washington Post*, January 10, 1996, p. D7.

98. Jane Scott, "Sit Back and Enjoy Bit of Old Front Row," *Cleveland Plain Dealer*, January 27, 1995, p. 18.

99. Interview with Irving Azoff, October 6, 2004.

100. Steven Young, "PCs Breaking Price Barrier," CNNMONEY, November 21, 1997, http://money.cnn.com/1997/11/21/technology/pcs_pkg/ (accessed March 29, 2005).

101. Jim Carlton, "Low—and Falling: PC Prices Just Smashed Through the $1,000 Barrier; and They Aren't Stopping," *Wall Street Journal*, June 15, 1998, p. R8.

102. Lan Xia, Kent B. Monroe, and Jennifer L. Cox, "The Price Is Unfair. A Conceptual Framework of Price Fairness Perceptions," *Journal of Marketing*, October 2004.

103. Sarah Maxwell, "What Makes a Price Increase Seem Fair?" *Pricing Strategy & Practice*, 3 (4), 1995, pp. 21–27.

104. Jesse McKinley, "For the Asking, a $480 Seat," *New York Times*, October 26, 2001, p. 1 (The Arts/Cultural Desk).

105. Tamar Lewin, "Students Find $100 Textbooks Cost $50, Purchased Overseas," *New York Times*, October 21, 2003, p. A1.

106. Ibid, p. A1.

107. Neil Strauss, "On Night Music Died, Many to Blame for Mayhem," *New York Times*, July 27, 1999, p. B5.

108. Sarah Lueck, "Ten Drug Makers Offer Price Breaks for Low Incomes—Discount Cards Will Make Cut Rates on Medicines Available to the Uninsured," *Wall Street Journal*, January 12, 2005, p. D4.

109. Sandra Naipaul and H.G. Parsa, "Menu Price Endings that Communicate Value and Quality," *Cornell Hotel & Restaurant Administration Quarterly*, February 1, 2001, volume 42, issue 1, pp. 26–37.

110. John Gourville and Dilip Soman, "Pricing and the Psychology of Consumption," *Harvard Business Review*, September 2002, pp. 91–96.

111. Eben Shapiro, "Price Lure of Private-Label Products Fail to Hook Many Buyers of Baby Food, Beer," *Wall Street Journal*, May 13, 1993, p. B1.

112. Alix M. Freedman, "A Price That's Too Good May Be Bad," *Wall Street Journal*, November 15, 1988.

113. Brian Wansink, Robert J. Kent, and Stephen J. Hoch, "An Anchoring and Adjustment Model of Purchase Quantity Decisions," *Journal of Marketing Research*, February 1998, volume XXXV, pp. 71–81.

114. Mark Minton, "Buy One Get One Free Sales Popular Among North Carolina Retailers," *News & Observer*, July 17, 2004.

115. Ann Zimmerman, "Behind the Dollar-Store Boom: A Nation of Bargain Hunters," *Wall Street Journal*, December 13, 2004, p. A1.

116. Laurie J. Flynn, "Apple Offers Music Downloads with Unique Pricing," *New York Times*, April 28, 2003, p. 2 (Business/Financial Desk).

117. For more information, please see: http://www.apple.com/pr/library/2003/may/05musicstore.html (accessed on March 29, 2005).

118. Neil Strauss, "Apple Finds Route for Online Music Sales," *New York Times*, May 29, 2003, p. 1 (Arts/Cultural Desk).

Acknowledgments

A friend of mine recently commented, "The happiest that I've ever seen you was when you were writing your book." He's right—it was a great period of my life. As I look back on this project, I realize how lucky I am to have good friends who supported me generously through the requisite struggles of making this book a reality. So, it's important for me to thank them for their help.

To echo what others have said about him, John Mahaney (executive editor of Crown Business) is an editor's editor. He's the best. This was the first time that I've worked with someone who was *always* right, and I learned a great deal from John. I'll miss the fun and productive working relationship we had.

I'm grateful to Gordon and Atsuko Paddison for their true friendship. They've always been there for me, and Gordon has gone out of his way to help me through some turbulent times.

ACKNOWLEDGMENTS

Linda "The Doctor" Van Gelder has been a genuine friend since our graduate school days. We've gone through a lot together, and she's my most trusted advisor. I treasure my friendship with Kathy Ivanciw and appreciate her support.

One of the biggest benefits from writing this book is the true friendship that I developed with Steve Szaraz. I've learned a lot from Steve, and I'm thankful to him for his continued support. George Eliades has been a great friend, and our discussions helped add some good natured humor into this book. I'm also very grateful to the following people who took the time to read the manuscript and weren't shy about telling me when I was wrong—the book is much clearer because of their comments: Bernie Jaworski, Kenneth Li, Craig Thompson, Eric Paley, Javier Colayco, and Marie Claire Guglielmo.

I also want to thank several of my professors at Cornell University, where the genesis of this book started sixteen years ago. Pat DeGraba is truly an economist's economist and a good friend. I'm always amazed by his ability to answer any economics question that I pose to him. Rob Masson has gone far beyond his duties as my committee chairman, and I appreciate his always being available for a new insight or advice. Bob Frank has continually encouraged my interest in pricing, and his innovative style of writing about economics is reflected in this book.

One of the most enjoyable parts of doing research is meeting people who unselfishly go out of their way to help you— I'm always amazed by their kindness and generosity. I learned a lot from the experiences and wisdom of the following people: Lloyd Hansen, Irving Azoff, Ron Tadross, Ron Robbins,

Doug Richters, Fritz Ahadi, Bill Stang, and Drew Atkinson. Thanks to Kent Monroe for sharing a forthcoming article that was helpful in pushing my thinking on fairness in pricing.

I am most grateful to the Batten Institute at the Darden Graduate School of Business, as well as Debbie Fisher and Bob Bruner for their friendship and generous help with my research. I'd like to thank Joe Fuller, as well as my many other friends and former colleagues at Monitor Group, for their good ideas, lively conversation, and active support for the writing of this book. Rafe Sagalyn has been an astute advisor and very supportive throughout this book project.

Finally, I'd like to thank the following people for their friendship—my life is a lot happier with them in it: Deborah Dupont, Katherine Jocz, Mike Yip, Dan Kim, Scott Becker, Bruce Weinberg, Chris Denton, and Omar Sadick.

Index

INDEX

INDEX

INDEX

About the Author

RAFI MOHAMMED is a director in the Cambridge office of Simon-Kucher & Partners, the prominent international pricing and strategy consulting firm. He has worked on pricing issues as an academic and government economist and now consults with companies in a wide range of industries on pricing strategy. His doctoral dissertation was published in the *Rand Journal of Economics*. Rafi worked on pricing issues at the Federal Communications Commission during the deregulation of the telecommunications industry, testified as a pricing expert at public-utility hearings, and was formerly a consultant at Monitor Group.

Rafi holds economics degrees from Boston University, the London School of Economics and Political Science, and Cornell University (Ph.D.) and has been a Batten Fellow at the University of Virginia's Darden Graduate School of Business. His website can be found at www.rafimo.com. Prior to joining Simon-Kucher & Partners, he was a consultant at Monitor Group.